COME UNTO THESE YELLOW SANDS

COME UNTO THESE YELLOW SANDS

ANGELA ✶ CARTER

BLOODAXE BOOKS

These plays were first broadcast by BBC Radio 3.

ISBN: 0 906427 66 5 hardback
      0 906427 67 3 paperback

First published 1985 by
Bloodaxe Books Ltd,
P.O. Box 1SN,
Newcastle upon Tyne NE99 1SN.

Bloodaxe Books Ltd acknowledges
the financial assistance of Northern Arts.

Typesetting by True North, Newcastle upon Tyne.

Printed in Great Britain by
Unwin Brothers Ltd, Old Woking, Surrey.

CONTENTS

List of Richard Dadd illustrations

The front cover shows a detail from **Come unto these Yellow Sands**. Cover design by Bloodaxe, with lettering by George Brown, after John Hassall's poster **Skegness Is So Bracing** 1909.

Special thanks for help given in the assembling of Richard Dadd illustrations for this book are due to Patricia Allderidge, Archivist to the Bethlem Royal Hospital and the Maudsley Hospital, and author of *The Late Richard Dadd 1817-1886* (Tate Gallery, 1974), to which acknowledgement is also made; and to the Paul Mellon Centre for Studies in British Art, to Graham Langton of the Tate Gallery and to Alice Munro-Faure of Sotheby's.

Preface

For me, writing for radio involves a kind of three-dimensional story-telling. Anyone, anywhere, who sits down to tell a story, from the narrator of fabulous epics in a pre-literate African community to a travelling salesman embarking on an anecdote in a bar, does so without the help of visual aids, and his or her narrative, however complex it might be thematically, will extend through time in, more or less, a straight line, its course determined by the characteristic copulas of the story: 'and then' . . . 'but then . . .' Radio may not offer visual images but its resources blur this linearity, so that a great number of things can happen at the same time. Yet, as with all forms of story-telling that are composed in words, not in visual images, radio always leaves that magical and enigmatic margin, that space of the invisible, which must be filled in by the imagination of the listener.

It is this necessary open-endedness of the medium, the way the listener is invited into the narrative to contribute to it his or her own way of "seeing" the voices and the sounds, the invisible beings and events, that gives radio story-telling its real third dimension, which is the space that, above all, interests and enchants me.

This is only one way out of many of using radio and none of them is the *right* way; all are possible ways—I'm not proselytizing for a pet method! This is, just, the way I like to use radio, not for creating dramas on a theatrical model so much as to create complex, many-layered narratives that play tricks with time. And, also, to explore ideas, although for me, that is the same thing as telling stories since, for me, a narrative is an argument stated in fictional terms.

Tricks with time—and also with place, for radio can move from location to location with effortless speed, using aural hallucinations to invoke sea-coast, a pub, a blasted heath, and can make extraordinary collage and montage effects beyond the means of any film-maker, not just because of the cost of that medium but also because the eye takes longer to register changing images than does the ear.

Even when the theatrical model exists in radio drama, when it is either an adaptation from the stage or bears a strong relation to the stage, it depends for its effects on the very absence of all the visual apparatuses that sustain the theatrical illusion. In a radio drama studio, the producer, the actors, the technical staff, create an illusion, literally, out of the air. Although there is a beautiful precision about the means available for the creation of that illusion. If you want to invoke a windy day on radio, you can specify just what kind of wind you want: summer, winter, spring winds, a gale, a breeze, wind in trees, in bushes, over water. Every wind in the world is stored away in the sound archives, somewhere on a disc. The resources are insubstantial but infinite. An Oriental market? Near East or Far East? At dawn, at noon, at dusk? If a Near Eastern market, with or without the muezzin?

The sound effects create their own system of signs for the ear, and language itself, the principal means of sustaining the radio drama illusion, may be richer and more evocative by far than that of real life, can release itself entirely from the conventions of everyday speech, can explore all kinds of rhetorical devices and linguistic tricks in order to do the work of sustaining an imaginary world.

Because of the absence of the visual image, radio drama need not necessarily be confined to the representations of things as they are. Since radio drama, or fiction for radio, or story-telling with radio, or any other use of radio at all other than for pure inform-ation-giving or opinion-giving, starts off from a necessary degree of stylisation, it has always attracted and continues to attract, the avant-garde. (Peter Redgrove's contemporary work for radio is scarcely conceivable in any other medium.) It is a medium that writers love.

There is also radio's capacity to render the inner voice, the subjective interpretation of the world . . . It is, *par excellence*, the medium for the depiction of madness; for the exploration of the private worlds of the old, the alienated, the lonely. As a result, plays about the inner lives of the mad, the old and the lonely have become almost Radio Three clichés, along with apocalypses and Kafkaesque existential confrontations of non-communication set in nameless, featureless places. I've been tempted, but always tried to avoid, these themes; although I've certainly done one play about a notable madman, I resisted the temptation to write it solely from his point of view.

Born in 1940, I was a child of the Radio Age—although, then, we still called it "the wireless"—as present-day children are the children of television. Weaned on the now defunct Children's Hour, one of the most potent memories of my childhood is that of a serial, always repeated around Christmas, made out of John Masefield's fantastic novel, *The Box of Delights*, with its cast list of piratical rats and time-travelling Renaissance philosophers, its ineffable atmosphere of snow and mystery. In an unselfconscious way, *The Box of Delights* used all the resources of radio to create what we now call "magic realism" and perhaps that long ago Children's Hour serial influenced me far more profoundly than I'd like to admit.

But I started writing for radio, myself, because of a sound effect. I made it quite by accident. Sitting in my room, pencil in hand, staring vacantly into space instead of getting on with whatever it was I was supposed to be doing, I ran the pencil idly along the top of the radiator. It made a metallic, almost musical rattle. It was just the noise that a long, pointed fingernail might make if it were run along the bars of a birdcage.

Now, I thought, what kind of person might have such fingernails? Why, a vampire, famed for their long, sharp fingernails (all the better to eviscerate you with!). Now, what kind of vampire would have both long, elegant fingernails and an elegant, gilt birdcage? A lady vampire, perhaps. I alliterated her. A lovely lady vampire. And she must be plucking those twanging, almost musical notes out of her birdcage because, like me, she was bored . . .

Bored, though, with what? With the endless deaths and resurrections she, the sleeping beauty who woke only to eat and then to sleep again, was doomed? A lovely lady vampire; last of her line, perhaps, locked up in her hereditary Transylvanian castle, and the bird in that gilded cage might be, might it not, an image of the lady herself, caged as she was by her hereditary appetites that she found both compulsive and loathsome.

So I laid aside the task I had in hand (now I misremember what it was), and researched vampires, and Transylvania. I invented for the lovely lady vampire, whom Anna Massey later gravely incarnated with such beautiful assurance, a hero out of the *Boys' Own* paper circa 1914, who would cure and kill her by the innocence of his kiss and then go off to die in a war that was more hideous by far than any of our fearful superstitious imaginings. I never thought of any other medium but radio all the time I was writing the script of the play, *Vampirella*. It *came* to me as radio, with all its images ready formed, in terms of words and sounds.

The script arrived at the BBC on the desk of the producer, Glyn Dearman, with whom I've worked ever since, and whose style, sensitivity and enthusiasm would irradiate dramatised readings of the London telephone directory. It was the happiest possible introduction to radio drama and I was forthwith hooked.

Later on, I took the script of *Vampirella* as the raw material for a short story, *The Lady of the House of Love*. It was interesting to see what would and would not work in terms of prose fiction. It was the discursive element in *Vampirella* that could not be contained in the short story. The narrative line of the short story did not have sufficient space to discuss the nature, real and imagined, of vampirism, nor did it have sufficient imaginative space to accommodate cameo guest appearances by the Scottish cannibal, Sawney Beane, with his bagpipes and his ravenous children, nor the unrepentant Parisian necrophile, Henri Blot. Even Vampirella's father, Count Dracula himself, was forced to bow out of a narrative that had become leaner, more *about* itself, less about its own resonances, and more consistent in tone.

In radio, it is possible to sustain a knife-edge tension between black comedy and bizarre pathos. ('Poor wee thing,' sighs Vampirella's governess over her charge's hideous longings.) This is because the rich textures of radio are capable of stating ambiguities with a dexterity over and above that of the printed word; the human voice itself imparts all manner of subteties in its intonations. So *The Lady of the House of Love* is a Gothic tale about a reluctant vampire; the radio play, *Vampirella*, is about vampirism as metaphor. The one is neither better nor worse than the other. Only, each is quite different.

Two of the scripts published here, *The Company of Wolves* and *Puss in Boots*, started off as short stories but these aren't adaptations so much as reformulations. As radio, both stories found themselves ending up much closer to specific types of genre—*The Company of Wolves* took on more of the characteristics of the pure horror story, became almost an exercise in genre until, now, it seems to me even a kind of homage to another radio fixture of my childhood, those mini-dramas of terror presented by Valentine Dyall as *The Man in Black*. The transformation of man into wolf is, of course, the work of a moment on radio and no werewolf make-up in the world can equal the werewolf you see in your mind's eye.

But *Puss in Boots* reverted very nearly to the exact form of the *commedia dell'arte* on which I'd modelled the original story in the first place. Puss was always Harlequin all the time, and Tabs was Columbine, while the young lovers, the old miser and the crone were all originally stock types from the early Italian comedy, from which the British popular form of pantomime is derived. That is why the whole thing is set in Bergamo, the town in Northern Italy where *commedia dell'arte* was especially cherished.

Recording *Puss in Boots* was the most fun I've ever had in a radio drama studio and the actors, somewhat breathlessly, concurred, although the production staff, faced with co-ordinating twanging bedsprings, heavy panting and Tchaikovsky's 1812 overture (with cannon) could not, at the time, see the funny side.

If *Puss in Boots* is an Old Comedy for radio, it is one that could only have been done in radio, not just because of the copulations, both feline and human, with which the script abounds, but because of the army of rats; and the acrobatics; and . . .

And the presence of the margin of the listener's imagination. Listening to the play when it went out over the air, I forgot I'd seen Andrew Sachs and Frances Jeator, Puss and Tabs respectively, acting in the studio; I heard the sharp, cunning voices of urban cats, unscrupulously charming as only cats who live by their wits can be. As for the pace, the spice, the *brio* of Glyn Dearman's production; well, I'd envisaged, shall we say, a balletic effect, hadn't I. A ballet in words. A ballet for radio?

Well, why not? We'd already done a picture gallery. Working on the fruitful paradox, that radio is the most visual of mediums because you cannot see it, I decided to paint some pictures in radio. Not, I hasten to add, my own pictures, but copies of somebody else's. I cheated a little, because they were not only narrative pictures, i.e. pictures that tell a story, but also pictures that could be construed as telling tales about the man who painted them. Who was a Victorian painter of fairy subjects named Richard Dadd, whose promising career terminated in his early twenties after, during an attack of paranoid schizophrenia, he cut his own father's throat. Dadd never recovered from his madness and spent the rest of his life in insane asylums; encouraged to continue painting, his style changed, although his subject matter unnervingly did not, and he produced the brilliant and disquieting canvasses on which his fame rests in the hospital that later became Broadmoor.

Come unto these Yellow Sands, my play about Dadd, isn't precisely story-telling for radio, nor is it art or cultural criticism, although there is a lot of that in the script. The contradiction between the kitsch content and the distorted style of the paintings of Dadd's madness, together with his archetypal crime of parricide, commited under a delusion of madness—committed in a state of not-knowing, in fact—seem to me expressions of the dislocation of the real relations of humankind to itself during Britain's great period of high capitalism and imperialist triumph in the nineteenth century, during Dadd's own long, alienated lifetime. And I don't see how it would have been possible for me to discuss Dadd in the way I wanted in any other medium than radio, with its ability to cross-cut from subjective to objective reality, from the inner, personal voice to the conflicting voices of those bearing witness to the diverse manifestations of that inner voice. From the apparently real to the patently imagined. From a Victorian mad-doctor discussing Dadd's case-notes to Oberon, King of the Fairies, discussing the marginalisation of folklore in the bourgeois period.

So *Come unto these Yellow Sands* isn't a documentary at all, nor, really, a play, but a piece of cultural criticism in the form of a documentary-based fiction in which the listener is invited inside some of Dadd's paintings, inside the 'Come unto these Yellow Sands' of the title and into that eerie masterpiece, 'The Fairy Feller's Master-Stroke', to hear the beings within it—the monsters produced by repression—squeak and gibber and lie and tell the truth.

On and off, I discuss with Glyn Dearman the idea of a play of the same kind about Jackson Pollock that would re-invent Pollock's paintings, and his times, in the same way as we re-invented Dadd's paintings for radio, with the aid, this time, of the BBC Radiophonic Workshop, perhaps. *That* would be a challenge.

Indeed, radio remains a challenging medium, because so much is possible in it. I write for radio by choice, as an extension and an amplification of writing for the printed page; in its most essential sense, even if stripped of all the devices of radio illusion, radio retains the atavistic lure, the atavistic power, of voices in the dark, and the writer who gives the words to those voices retains some of the authority of the most antique tellers of tales.

ANGELA CARTER

TITANIA SLEEPING

PUCK

These tiny, charming, antic creatures, scarce bigger, some of them, than a dewdrop, contort themselves in all manner of quaint dispositions. Some puff out their cheeks to fill the trumpets of the sweet woodbine with music for my nocturnal serenades, others finger arpeggios upon their own noses, which have whimsically acquired the shape of clarinets. Outside my enchanted slumber, nymphs dance.

Peak fairy music briefly.

The tranquil and timeless light of fairyland, the quintessential distillation of moonlight, falls on the bare shoulders of my two attendants and suffuses the white, rosy-shadowed velvet with which my own succulent limbs are upholstered.

My succulent yet immaterial limbs.

Music distorts.

Above my grotto, there is a kind of arch formed by an interesting monster with a great many leathern wings.

Titania yawns; settles back to sleep again; tittering of fays. Fade tittering and music.

MALE NARRATOR. The same year, Dadd exhibited a companion piece to his Titania at the Society of British Artists. Oil on canvas, twenty three and a quarter inches by twenty three and a quarter inches. **Puck** . . .

Brisk plucking notes into brisker fairy music.

PUCK. (*Leaping up from nowhere.*) . . . whom he painted as a plump, white, juicy child seated on a toadstool of a botanically imprecise description with, directly above my head, a bindweed blossom looking not unlike a particularly vulgar satin lampshade, because it dangles a fringe of pendant dewdrops for all the world like glass beads. Around my little pedestal, which looks far too frail to support my Bacchic corpulence, dance dozen of those tiny nudes, dozens of them.

Fairy music speeds up behind following:

Dozens of them, jiggering about with positively frenetic abandon, whirling like dervishes, dervishes . . .

And I am bathed in the coolest, purest light, the light of another world.

Beginning of a rustling and tittering, the sounds of the stirring of a horrid, goblin crowd. Lose music behind them.

MALE NARRATOR. In the same year, Dadd exhibited 'Fairies Assembling to Hold Their Revels', now lost, at Manchester.

Louder mutterings.

PUCK. Ravishingly pretty . . . but so much, so very much prettiness suggests the presence of far too many ugly beings gibbering away behind the painted screen where he pushed them—

SCOTS GOBLIN. You may find me in Glen Etive, night coming on, there is my one hand out of my chest, my one leg out of my arse, my one eye in the middle of my forehead and I bode nae good to nae man, I can tell you.

YORKSHIRE GOBLIN. Sithen that keeps away from t'marl-pit or raw-head-and-bloody-bones will catch you! I sit on a mound of fresh-gnawed bones and my wounds never stop bleeding and I'm always wi' me weather eye open for fresh meat . . .

WEST COUNTRY GOBLIN. I have gurt horns and gurt claws and gurt red 'ot eyes; when I howl, somebody is dying.

Fade mutterings behind following:

PUCK. From all these pictures of fairyland for which young Dadd received so much praise, he chose to leave out the pharisees, the trolls, those shapeless somethings always at your left shoulder that manifest themselves like bad breath, the hags, the shape-shifters, the banshees, the hobs and lobs and all the nasty little demons who exist at the corner of the eye, in the cobwebbed back passages of the mind.

Sound of footsteps trooping into lecture theatre; squeaks, gibbers, honking—not a normal crowd.

(*Officious.*) Settle down, please, settle down . . . emanations of the id to the back of the room, apparitions from the unconscious and preconscious in the gallery. Pre-Christian survivals, fertility symbols, nightmares and ghouls in the pews to the right, death-signs, stormwarnings, to the left. Oedipal fantasies in the front row, please.

Squeaks, gibbers, objects being thrown.

And I'll thank you poltergeists to keep a firm hold on your impulses during the lecture.

OBERON. (*Clears throat, rustles papers.*)

Chairs squeak, hubbub gradually subsides.

PUCK. Bugs, long-legged beasties and things that go bump in the night, it is my pleasure and privilege to present to you, summoned here from the vasty deep tonight, Oberon, king of the fairies, fallen angel locked out of both hell and heaven, leader of the wild hunt etc. etc. etc . . .

Applause.

OBERON. Thank you, friends, thank you.

Rustles papers, coughs.

The vogue for paintings of fairy subjects during the mid-Victorian period might be regarded as the manifestation of a compensatory "ideology of innocence" in the age of high capitalism, a period when the relations of man with his kind were increasingly under stress and the art which reflected these relations became increasingly fraudulent.

Hobgoblin chorus of cheers. Hear hear! Well said!

The primitive superstitions of the countryside, the ancient lore born on the wrong side of the blanket to religious faith, could not survive in the smoke, the stench, the human degradation, the poverty, the cholera, the tuberculosis, of the great cities which the industrial revolution had created.

Here, the poor were stripped of everything, even of their irrational dreads, and the external symbols of their dreams and fears—the wraiths of nightmare—were utilised to provide their masters with a decorative margin of the "quaint", the "fanciful" and the "charming" upon the printed pages of lives that had no imaginative richness of their own.

Bangings of cans, squeaks, cheers.

The richly sexual symbolism of aspects of the mythology of the "wee folk" was buried so deeply beneath the muffling layers of repression and the oppression of women that the fairies were often depicted on these canvasses in states of virtually complete undress, of active nudity . . .

Wolf-whistle; shushings.

. . . at a period when formal art treated the nude with kid gloves, in the passive mood.

It might be said of these fairy painters, as Hamlet says of Ophelia:

> Death and affliction, even hell itself,
> She turns to favour and to prettiness.

This realm of fictive faery served as a kitschified repository for fancies too savage, too dark, too voluptuous, fancies that were forbidden the light of common Victorian day *as such*. If the reality of the artist could not accommodate itself to that of the world of iron, of steam, of labour, of strife, he retreated to the consolation of the midsummer fairies without the least idea of the true nature of such creatures in any symbolic schema worth its salt. The enchanting light that bathes these whimsical canvasses falsifies not only experience but imagination itself.

Imagination, severed from reality, festers. The beautiful thought in a world of pain is, in itself, a crime.

Buzzes, groans, shrieks.

The Victorian fairyland is a place that not only never existed but also served no imaginative function except that of diversion, of the prim titillation of a jaded fancy. It represents a kind of pornography of the imagination.

In this pre-sexual fairyland, dreams may indeed come true. (*He's working up to a lecturer's joke.*) And I hardly need remind our Oedipal friends here in the front row what happens when dreams come true in reality!

Laughter; applause. A high wind rises, the same wind that will blow when Dadd goes to see the sphinx; Oberon's voice is blown away by the wind, gets smaller and smaller from now on, until it fades away altogether.

Fairyland, for Henry Howard, and Dickie Doyle, and Arthur Huskisson, and Richard Dadd, was what one might term the "pastoral exotic", a wilful evasion of the real conditions of life in the insensate industrial towns such as the Manchester of Engels, during the era of imperialist expansion of . . .

Fade wind.

FEMALE NARRATOR. In July of the year 1842 Richard Dadd set out on a grand tour of the historic and picturesque ruins of the Middle East as the companion of Sir Thomas Phillips, a former mayor of Newport, Monmouthshire. Phillips, a solicitor, had been knighted for the part he played in putting down the Chartists. Phillips hired Dadd as an artist, to make him an album of water-colour drawings as a souvenir of the trip.

MALE NARRATOR. The last picture Dadd painted before he set sail with his patron was titled: **Come unto these Yellow Sands**.

Distant singing, as at opening; faint sound of waves.

FEMALE NARRATOR. A wild saraband on a deserted beach, at evening.

PUCK. Whirling like dervishes! Like dervishes!

FEMALE NARRATOR. The grand chain of dancers partially conceal their nakedness with swathes of chiffon that drifts to reveal nipples, muscles, sinews that, since they belong to the fairy folk, may be depicted in all the forbidden splendour of authentic flesh because the fairies do not exist. The pleasures of the flesh, rendered insubstantial as dream.

The rising moon applies a coat of mother o' pearl to the ambiguously sexed beings. Half the eldritch company float in a great curlicue upon the air, immune to gravity, while the leaders of the dance pass through an arch of rock as through the eye of a needle.

Music fades; waves rise.

The waves break on the barren shore.

SIR THOMAS PHILLIPS. All in all, all went splendidly at first. After we had "done" Europe most comprehensively—I was an indefatigable tourist, I assure you—we left Greece to sail for Smyrna, and, once landed . . .

Waves recede.

. . . set out in a caravan across landscapes of most savage splendour.

Fade in desert: bells, hooves.

The untamed wilderness spread out for our delight like a glorious picture-book.

DADD. We would stop at some wild, uninhabited place, always in the open, under the stars; we would put down our mattresses, have the mules unloaded, the cook would light the fire . . .

Crackling of flames, clank of cooking and eating utensils, muttering of men.

PHILLIPS. Atrocious food, of course. The soup, often, nothing but raw onions in it. And rice, perhaps a stringy fowl boiled to ribbons, a few pots of sour milk . . .

DADD. And the light always gone by the time the caravan halted, dammit, so that my pencil could scarcely keep pace with my impressions by the flickering of our camp fire . . .

Crossfade back to desert; hooves, bells.

Then back into the saddle at dawn and jolt, jolt, jolt across another plain of rocks. The sky burning, now blue, now green, above an arid yet sublime terrain . . . and I, accustomed to the sweet English watercolour meadows and the lovely realm of fancy, of poetry . . .

PHILLIPS. From Smyrna to Constantinople to Bodrum to the great ruins at Lycia . . .

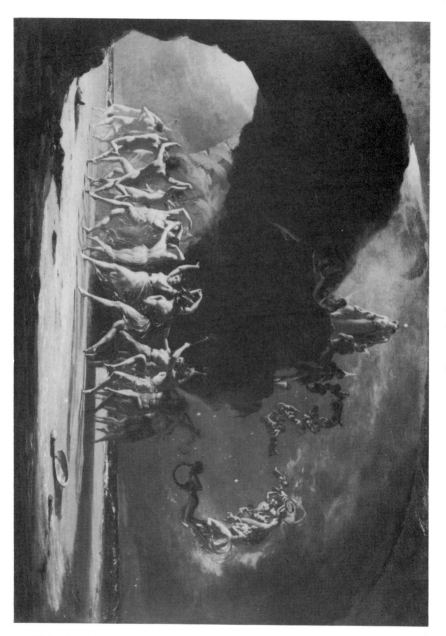

COME UNTO THESE YELLOW SANDS

DADD. . . . I, all unprepared for the stark light, the wild people, was precipitated into a landscape not dissimilar to that of the infernal regions . . .

PHILLIPS. . . . to Beirut, to Damascus . . .

Muezzin which brings in background of Damascus.

DADD. At evening, as we approached the city, the domes and minarets seemed to be embroidered on a sky of flushed satin; a scene of such ethereal loveliness that it lodged in my memory like a kind of grace, amongst much that I found strangely troubling to my spirits. For nothing was as I could have imagined it, all threw my nerves into a state of tremendous agitation. Can men truly live in such a different way to us?

PHILLIPS. When the circumstances of our travels permitted it, I urged my young companion to sketch the picturesque and exotic spectacles of our travels.

Bring in screeching and wailing of mourners.

DADD. In Damascus, we chanced to see a funeral procession, I had never seen anything like it, nothing . . . the mourners screeching, the women tearing their clothes, pouring dust from the road by the handful on their veils . . . so that they seemed demented rather than grief-stricken. And then, the dervishes . . .

Crossfade to dervishes.

And then, the dervishes—a group of those holy men who dance until they are possessed by their god; they whirled and whirled until they fell, exhausted, lips rimed with froth, a wild saraband.

Crossfade to hubbub of eastern bazaar.

In Damascus, walking about the maze of alleys, I came upon a *camel*, poor beast, great, lolloping, starveling brute, who had fallen in the street. Fallen and, I think, broken a leg. Fallen, with all the baggage upon him, in a street so narrow he quite blocked the traffic . . .

Peak eastern hubbub, cries and down .

His driver, in his filthy robes, beat the beast but it would not, could not rise. And then, oh horror! they came with axes and with knives and lopped off all its living limbs, as one might lop off the limbs of a tree . . . As it lay there in the intolerable heat of noon, heat so intense it seemed all nature itself might faint with it . . . and the blood sprang out and flowed away down the gutters, mingling with the foul odours of the city . . . and still the wretched camel lived, it shrieked and writhed most fearfully . . .

Camel shriekings, cries, blows.

. . . and still lived until at last they . . . slit its throat . . . and then they could carry it away piecemeal, you understand, bit by bit. And in that way, the street was cleared.

Fade background.

Horrible! Horrible!

Bring in faint wind.

PHILLIPS. In November, we arrived at last in Egypt.

DADD. We had taken a boat to Alexandria. During the brief respite from these savage countries that the sea afforded me, I had felt a lightening of the spirits, the oppression which I had experienced among those intolerable marvels lifted a little. Yet, when we disembarked at Alexandria, although I was consumed by a scarcely tolerable anguish of despair as soon as my feet touched the ancient earth of Egypt, I also felt, at the same time, a sense of *homecoming*, of arriving at a destination that was my destiny, and, in its inescapable quality, this sensation was especially . . . atrocious.

The vast, pitiless, antique land welcomed me as if I was its son.

Crossfade to bazaar behind following:

PHILLIPS. So we stopped a while in Cairo. Good beds at last, clean linen. The hospitable consul provided decent grub. My young companion browsed about the bazaar, searching out souvenirs, antiquities . . .

Jangling of a shop bell—take down bazaar background.

SHOPKEEPER. Effendi?

DADD. The meanest merchant in the bazaar looks like a Sultan in an eastern fairy tale . . .

SHOPKEEPER. I knew immediately I saw him that this young man would buy anything I chose to sell him.

In my little shop in the bazaar in Cairo, I did profitable business with many interesting foreign visitors throughout the entire nineteenth century. Artists of all kinds patronised me; it was no less a one than Victor Hugo himself who gave business a tremendous boost, first of all, with his 'Les Orientales' of 1829.

MALE NARRATOR.
Ma dague d'un sang noir à mon côté ruisselle
Et ma hache est pendue à l'arcon de ma selle.

SHOPKEEPER. My dagger drips black blood beside me and my axe hangs from the pommel of my saddle. Exactly. Hugo wished to purchase projections of exotic violence; I supplied them. In the drawing-rooms of Paris, Lyons, London, Manchester, the dreams rose up in cursive blue smoke, like incense, from the open pages of handsomely illustrated albums. Pierre Loti, an afficionado of the quaint, a regular customer . . . he was pleased to take off my hands a rose-water sprinkler formerly in the possession of the aunt of the Prophet. (*Giggles.*) And I sold one or two particularly succulent trinkets—I especially recall a back-scratcher in the shape of the eyebrow of Ra, removed from the tomb of Queen Nefertiti herself—to Gérard de Nerval, when he stayed in Cairo in 1849 . . . de Nerval, another madman.

Ah, you strike a hard bargain, effendi!

Cash register.

You would have thought the East had turned their brains.

The English were less flamboyant and more obsessed, preferring the secrecy of watercolour to the privacy of oils. I remember certain furtive visits of a curious fat man, Edward Lear . . . Towards the end of the century, Lord Leighton was so struck with the Orient that he went home and built a Moorish hall in Kensington for which I was able to supply a number of tasselled hangings and bead curtains at absolutely cut-throat prices . . .

Cash register.

What's this? (*To inaudible voice over his shoulder.*) What? You want my lecture on orientalism?

Coughs, clears throat. Crossfade to rustling of lecture theatre audience.

My lecture on orientalism . . . are you attending? Very well.

Throughout the nineteenth century, the Orient exercised a magnetic attraction upon the European middle class, to whom my distinguished visitors purveyed the aesthetic, the sense of style, the taste. Emergent in the seventeenth, rising in the eighteenth, the middle class spent the nineteenth century consolidating itself. It looked at the smoky evidence of the Industrial Revolution that had nurtured its prosperity and turned away its face. These rich dissatisfied men and women saw the world they had made in their own image and they did not like it, although they depended on it to stay alive. They wanted to be taken out of themselves, you understand, but *not for long.*

So tourism was born.

But they soon realised they could hire their artists to do their travelling for them, and so need not hazard the flies, the heat, the diarrhoea and so forth. The European middle class drank deep of the savage splendours of the East, the pious grandeurs of the the Holy Land, without stirring a step from their drawing-rooms.

OBERON. . . . a compensatory ideology of innocence . . .

SHOPKEEPER. (*Tetchy.*) No, no, no, no! Innocence? Never! These were the lands of the harem, of the assassin, of the naked blonde slave-girl in the market . . . the cult of the exotic was a compensatory ideology of sensuality, of mystery, of violence. Of the *forbidden*, which the customers of my customers could enjoy vicariously, without any danger of their souls.

The Orient held an especial attraction for those uneasy in their spirits.

Crossfade back to interior shop with distant bazaar.

DADD. Good morning.

SHOPKEEPER. I gave him a little cup of hot, sweet coffee with cardoman in it; they adored such details.

And now, let me display my treasures . . . objets d'art, curios, little items from the tombs of the pharoahs such as beads of faience and cornelian; rings of jasper, faience and gold; lapis lazuli scarabs blue as the sky, effendi, and mounted in gold . . . tiny figures of the gods . . .

DADD. Gods who ruled the sky before Christ was born . . .

SHOPKEEPER. Or, perhaps, one of these small rolls of papyrus . . .

Unwraps.

. . . removed from the grave-wrappings of the dead, inscribed with chapters from the Kitab-el-mayyitum . . .

DADD. The Kitab-el . . .

SHOPKEEPER. We call it, The Book of the Dead.

DADD. And I saw before me messages from the beginning of time, in an inscrutable script formed of hawks and serpents, full moons and crescents, undulations as of the frozen wave.

SHOPKEEPER. 'The sky burns for you, the earth trembles for you, before the birth of the god.'

DADD. Fearful, wonderful . . .

SHOPKEEPER. . . . 'Hail to thee, O Bull of the Land of the West. I am one of those gods who cut in pieces the enemies of Osiris.'

DADD. (*Shuddering sigh.*) The West?

SHOPKEEPER. The Land of the Dead. 'Behold, Osiris!'

DADD. And the very mention of the holy name, Osiris, made the hair upon my nape stand upright, a shiver of electric dread and holy expectation ran through me . . .

SHOPKEEPER. Osiris, the King of the Dead, who weighs your heart, effendi.

    Cash register which cuts bazaar and returns us to lecture hall.

And so we earned our bread by the sale of the mummified remains of antiquity and our customers made of it exactly what they pleased. We were not responsible for their fantasies about us. And could they not turn the pages of the magic book of our lives as soon as they got tired of us?

    Pause.

PHILLIPS. After so much sight-seeing, I yearned for a spot of sport. I would go banging away at crocodiles along the Nile while my young companion took himself off with his easel . . .

    Fade in desert.

DADD. The desert starts at the gates of Cairo, the desert, mother of mirages, where the light is white as if the sand had scoured the polished metal of the sun white . . .

PHILLIPS. . . . he'd blacken page after page of his sketchbook, zeal enough for a dozen artists, such enthusiasm he'd scarcely take shelter even during the fiercest portion of the noonday sun . . .

DADD. . . . white heat, that pulsed . . .

PHILLIPS. Scribble, scribble as if he were making sketches enough to serve him for the rest of his lifetime!

DADD. And often, after a day's sketching, I lay down at night with my imagination so full of wild vagaries that I really and truly doubted of my own sanity . . .

PHILLIPS. Took the boat down to Thebes, good shooting along the banks of the Nile, our destination—the Sphinx. Memorable spectacle, truly memorable.

Thin, high wind rises.

DADD. The sphinx it was herself who whispered to me what Oedipus knew. I went to see her, she was crouching in the middle of the dead sea of sand, attended by three inscrutable pyramids. I saw her lips move but you had to listen very hard to hear what she was saying and at first I could not believe what she told me; her message or prophecy cast me into the pit where terror lives.

Wind blows through the rest of the speech.

I prayed to Osiris for his guidance, guidance from this most antique and therefore most authentic of deities, for the world had resolved itself around me into weird and dreadful forms.

Wind fades leaving desert background.

PHILLIPS. A touch of the sun, poor Dadd, a nasty touch of sunstroke. Been doing too much; overtaxed himself, out in the sun all day . . . Delirium; babbling away about I don't know what.

DADD. Visitation of the godhead in a beam of white light . . .

PHILLIPS. . . . asked me to look into his mouth, to see if there was a *green feather* on his tongue. And then he saw men with heads of dogs and cow-headed women in the room . . .

DADD. I am come to judgement, I am come to judgement . . .

PHILLIPS. Indeed, I was quite concerned about the poor fellow but, mercifully, a day's complete rest, a good night's sleep and a good English breakfast of tea and toast and boiled eggs—thanks to the British consul!—and he seemed right as rain again.

DADD. Although I recovered from the ghastly hallucinations that my attack of sunstroke procured me, they left me terribly, terribly fearful . . . that I might hearken to those voices of the messengers of death, that I might allow myself . . . to believe in their existence . . .

PHILLIPS. Homeward bound, old boy! From Alexandria, by ship to Malta—

Bring in sea and creaking of rigging.

DADD. And I grew afraid that . . . I might lose . . . my reason . . .

Creaking of rigging and sound of conviviality, bottles clinking.

PHILLIPS. A queen and, by jove, an ace!

DADD. And I scrutinised the Book of the Dead again and again, and always my eye fell upon those symbols that the merchant had told me signified: 'The Great God aboard the Divine Ship' . . .

Burst of laughter from Phillips.

PHILLIPS. My game again, captain!

DADD. (*New, brisk, self-confident voice.*) Under a spare sail slung amidships for a canopy, my worthy benefactor and the ship's captain play all day at cards, sipping thick tumblerfuls of cloudy arak that turn my gut when I try to drink it. Look, he deals—

Slap of cards on table; Phillips snorts with glee.

DADD. He deals the devil's picture books. And I do believe . . . that his tailcoat . . . conceals his tail . . .

Laughter of card-players.

PHILLIPS. And it's my game, again!

Gathers cards together.

DADD. And as they played and poured more and yet more arak, I was seized with the conviction that the stake of the game was nothing less than that sea-captain's soul. The point of my pencil snapped in two; I could sketch no more that day! The world burst into fragments of ferocious light and fire whirled about me. With expressions of the most vicious and deceitful concern, my so-called benefactor came to me where I lay struck down on the deck—

PHILLIPS. Dadd! Dadd, I say!

DADD. Take your hands off me, you devil—

Scuffling which fades behind following:

PHILLIPS. We got him to his cabin, at last, sponged him down with cool water, left him in a dark room and out he came at sun-down, full of apologies. Delicate constitution, of course, artistic temperament.

Fade sea.

So we made our way to Rome . . .

Fade in crowd noises.

. . . where, to my consternation, outside the Vatican . . .

DADD. As soon as the Pope, the Holy Father, stepped out upon the balcony, raising his hand in satanic benediction on that obscenely ululating crowd, I understood my sacred duty; I sprang forward—

Consternation; scuffling.

But the servants of the Prince of Darkness laid their hands upon me and restrained me.

Fade scuffling and crowd.

PHILLIPS. When we reach Paris, I shall make quite certain that Dadd sees a doctor.

DADD. Although he posed as my benefactor and a father to me, this man, this Phillips, all the time wove the ghastliest plans for the perdition of my spirit that would have to come to fruition in Paris had I not given the slip to this emissary of the devil, to post directly home—

Fade in Victorian London street noises; cab-wheels, street cries.

FRITH. I must confess to you, sir, that since your son returned from the East, he's been behaving in such an odd way that I hardly like to have him visit my studio.

ROBERT DADD. He is a little overtired from his travels; the exertion, his delicate nerves . . . and is he not painting away in his studio, after all? Has he not sent paintings to the Liverpool Academy? Is he not hard at work?

Fade street noises.

MALE NARRATOR. A watercolour from this period, 'Dead Camel', now lost, has been described as 'a ghastly little invention of desert-horror framed in by demons such as his distempered brain alone could devise'.

Fade in room acoustic.

LANDLADY. Well, sir, I can tell you that during those three months after the poor young man's return from abroad, he lodged in my house at Newman Street, London, and in and out he would go, about his business, scowling furiously and, sometimes, suddenly grimacing and showing his teeth in such a wild, distracted way that I grew quite frightened of him. And his clothes spotted and dirtied with paint something dreadful; but then, I thought, he is an artist . . .

He told me, did he not, never to set foot in his rooms, neither to clean them up nor to bring him water even for his own ablutions. Never disturb my apartments! he said, with vehemence enough to scare you witless; for, he says, I'm engaged in researches upon the subject of the enemies of the *Almighty*, he says, and my rooms are now sanctuaries for the Great God Osiris, of whom, whilst in Egypt, I was permitted to become a devotee.

Well, I have had strange ones in this house, and, since he paid his rent regular, I thought no more of it.

Indeed, great cases of books and curios now arrived for him that he had purchased in Egypt but I never set eyes on the contents of those chests until after the accident, for he unpacked them in perfect secrecy.

And, yes . . . he said we should give him nothing to eat, for, according to his religion, he must prepare his own diet.

Cracking of eggshells.

DADD.   Ex ova omnia, all things come from the egg. I shall eat nothing but eggs, the little emblems of eternity, round . . . with a germ of new life in the middle, and I shall eat eggs until I become eternal . . .

LANDLADY. So that, after the accident, we came to clean out his place at last and found eggshells everywhere, ground into the carpet, eggshells in the grate, eggshells on all the tome upon tome of lore about Ancient Egypt and how I pitied his poor solitary meals! But the walls were covered with a tremendous number of drawings of his friends that he had held most dear and all of them, in these pictures, had their throats cut . . .

ROBERT DADD. Rest and quiet. He has not yet recovered from the effects of the sun. Rest, quiet, country air . . .

Fade in birdsong.

MALE NARRATOR. (*Cool voice.*) On 28th August Dadd called on his father and asked him to go to the country with him.

Fade birdsong behind following:

Out walking in Cobham Park, Richard Dadd killed his father with a spring-knife he had brought with him for that purpose, under the delusion that his father was the devil and he himself the incarnation of the god, Osiris.

Pause.

FEMALE NARRATOR. He escaped to France, where he was committed to an asylum after attempting to kill a fellow passenger in a carriage. Almost a year later, he was extradited back to England. On 22nd August 1844 he was admitted to the criminal lunatic department of Bethlem Hospital. From that date, Richard Dadd's experience may be termed, posthumous. He was then twenty-six years old.

Silence.

FRITH. A catastrophe sudden, overwhelming and absolute. He— (*Voice breaks off, overcome.*)

Fiddle tentatively tuning up.

DADD. Far . . .

CRAZY JANE. Far?

DADD. . . . away . . .

Country fiddle playing old tune.

CRAZY JANE. You don't want for recreation, then; they let you have your old fiddle, to make a bit of music with.

DADD. Far away from this rock and castle of seclusion . . .

Fade fiddle; writing noises.

DOCTOR. As his physician, I feel compelled to report that his delusion remains fixed and immovable, his conversation sometimes exceedingly unpleasant. Colours and canvasses have been provided for him.

CRAZY JANE. Watercolours, pastels—oils, even. They let you paint your pictures, then.

FEMALE NARRATOR. He soon resumed painting. But his work suffered a sea change. As if his delusion were an ocean in which he had drowned, full fathom five—or, more deeply still; drowned, fathom upon unimaginable fathom, lost to us more profoundly than if he had been dead in an abyss of loss, the cruellest of all losses, the loss of reason.

In this dreadful isolation, his painting took on an hallucinatory clarity. It underwent a kind of magical petrification. In these strange canvasses, the rules of time and space and perspective have undergone a subtle transformation and there is no effect of either depth or movement. As if everything had stopped still, stock fast, frozen in time at the moment that the fatal blow was struck, the crime of Oedipus committed that exiled him forever from the company of those who acknowledge a distinction between inside and outside.

Yet there is an almost miraculous intensification of colour, as if he no longer dipped his brush in natural pigment but in crushed mineral substances brighter and more shining than those used by painters who inhabit *this* world.

And his work become enormously small, as if the fairies who

invaded the most remarkable canvasses of his earliest years of solitude were now directing the infinite littleness of the arabesques of the tip of his brush, as if, indeed, he were not painting fancies but, rather, real sitters from a perfectly material realm of concrete dream.

MALE NARRATOR. **Contradiction: Oberon and Titania**, oil on canvas, twenty four inches by twenty nine and a half inches, painted by Dadd between 1854 and 1858 for Dr William Charles Hood, physician superintendent of Bethlem Hospital.

FEMALE NARRATOR. He shaped the canvas into an oblate spheroid, like the shape of the world in the Mercator projection. Or the shape of a tear laid on its side.

TITANIA. And he has learned some respect for the Queen of the Fairies. Now I dwarf my court!

Thumping footsteps; humming, buzzing.

Here come I, Titania, with my gigantic stride! How big I've grown, since the time he took my picture when I was sleeping in the glade. I tower over my fairy subjects like Gulliver in Lilliput; I trample them underfoot—

Particularly thumping footstep; tiny fairy scream.

There! I've flattened her, that winged creature no bigger than my little finger who nestled in the flower bell.

Insects buzzing, clicking of cicadas etc.

Fairyland buzzes with the whirr of tiny wings; fays like gnats, like midges, like flies.
    He has lost his sense of scale. If this enormous butterfly is as big as I, then it is twice the size of the hairy-chested, horned and bearded fairy centaur who leaps across the violets at the viewer's right, drawing upon me a bow in a fairy assassination attempt that suggests Mr Dadd has left a little signature of murder, almost invisibly, in a corner, in order to tease . . .
    Such a crowded composition, what overpopulation in fairyland! And the noise, the bustle . . .

Peak background and down.

CONTRADICTION. OBERON AND TITANIA

Huge blue trumpets of the hallucinatory morning glory roll round my feet; they have the fragile solidity of painted tin, like the horns of old gramophones . . .

Tinny sound of cylinder gramophone playing Mendelssohn's 'Midsummer Night's Dream' music.

TITANIA. I have grown very brown, As if my skin had been burned by hotter suns than coaxed his cold kingcups and lilies of the valley out of the earth. The curving petals of these flowers have the waxen and unnatural precision of immortelles, everlasting flowers, graveyard bouquets. They cannot fade because they never grew. Flowers the yellowish-white of fangs.

OBERON. He has decided to give to me, Oberon, the fierce, proud air of an Arab chieftain or a Kurdish brigand. No doubt he took my features from some sketch or other of his travels. Observe my eaglish beak of a nose, my fine, crisply curling black beard. And Dadd has dressed me in a fringed tunic of Middle-Eastern provenance and sandals of archaic design. I clasp the arm of my pretty page; horsemen small enough to pass through the eye of a needle ceaselessly parade behind me.

Tiny horns and drums above the tinny gramophone music.

The leaves of the plants are flat as palm fans, they might be made of beaten metal, their edges look as if they could cut you. Cruel things occur diminutively in the undergrowth, which is a complicated web of metal vines in which the wee folk are trapped.

No wind stirs or ever could this frozen grove. Time does not exist, here. She and I confront one another in a durationless present.

TITANIA. Dew, dew everywhere. It hangs in lucid drops endlessly about to fall, never to fall, from feathery grasses that curl above us, dew blisters the depthless surfaces of the leaves and flowers, dew like heavy glass beads hanging on the folds of our clothes. But the dew isn't wet; it won't drench us, the dew drips like tears but tears that have dropped from a crystal eye, heavy, solid, mineral, glittering, unnatural. And the earth under the sharp embroidery of the flowers is hard as ship's biscuit.

During this speech, apart from the tinny Mendelssohn, sounds such as: tweeting of electronic birds; plop of a single raindrop; squeaks; buzzes. The music hiccups and begins to repeat itself.

OBERON. Ill-met by moonlight, proud Titania!

TITANIA. What, jealous Oberon!

OBERON. Ill-met by moonlight, proud Titania!

TITANIA. What, jealous Oberon!

OBERON. Ill-met by moonlight, proud Titania!

TITANIA. What, jealous Oberon!

Voices, still repeating themselves, fade. Cackling of hobs rises.

CHANGELING. There is no time in fairyland. Of his visit there, the changeling remembers nothing but pleasant music and returns, a youth, still, to find his mother dead, his cottage tumbled into ruin, the acorn his father planted for him on the day when he was born grown into an oak and his name forgotten . . .

OBERON. Because time does not pass in these wards of absence, everything acquires the quality of still life—

CHANGELING. Or, as the French say, nature morte.

TITANIA. (*Rich, full.*) Yet what can you imagine lovelier than fairyland?

Tittering of fays.

CRAZY JANE. They do say the fairy women have beautiful faces, indeed; but when you look at them from the back, it turns out they are hollow. Quite hollow. Like jelly moulds wi' no jelly in 'em.

LANCASHIRE GOBLIN. Shriker I am, that pads behind thee in the dark night and shrieks—

Scream.

FEMALE GOBLIN. Black Annis has a blue face and great teeth and she will come and *gobble you up* . . .

Fade background.

MALE NARRATOR. Somebody took Dadd's photograph as he was at work upon this picture.

FEMALE NARRATOR. He turns towards the camera an immense, haunted, shaggy, bearded head.

His eyes, opaque, as if they had been put out by pearls.

Fade in asylum acoustic.

DOCTOR. Very charming, very charming, Mr Dadd. And now, perhaps, you could paint one like that just for me—a special commission for your good doctor, who treats you kindly and would like to keep your mind upon the harmless fairies, give you no time to brood upon questions of antique theology.

MALE NARRATOR. The picture usually considered Dadd's master-piece, **The Fairy Feller's Master-Stroke**, took nine years to complete. Oil on canvas, twenty one and quarter inches by fifteen and a half inches.

THE FAIRY FELLER'S MASTER-STROKE

FEMALE NARRATOR. The texture is as thickly embossed as that of petit point; it looks as though the picture might be read with the fingertips, like braille. The composition is of the utmost complexity, something is going on in every centimetre. And yet a frozen calm holds all the weird actors still. The picture offers a scene from a narrative just before the conclusion; it illustrates a story that has not begun and therefore cannot end, it tells an anecdote the point of which is never made.

Full in babble of fairy voices.

RUSTIC GOBLIN. Do 'ee but strike the blow, master! Do 'ee but strike the blow!

CRAZY JANE. See, there's the young man with the gurt axe—

FEMALE NARRATOR. On a wee section of moonlit hill, an innumerable horde of beings have gathered together to witness the fairy feller, our hero, strike a nut with an axe. There are huge daisies above their heads and about their feet. Each petal of the moon-drenched daisies stands out with an hallucinated clarity and the little flowers are white as if made from white metal. Not silver, whiter than silver. And they emit such a luminous gleam they seem of themselves to illuminate this crowded brake where the fairies come.

Babble rises.

Each grain of sand is as distinctly visible to the eye as it would be to the eye of god.

FAIRY FELLER. Now I raise my trusty weapon in my good right hand—

Squeaks; buzzings; chatterings.

Such a troupe gathered here to see my fatal blow, you can't count them. Here we have, all gathered together, soldiers, gypsies, fiddlers in rags and tags and scarlet jackets, masons and carpenters in their aprons come here a-riding on mice, a deputation of the famous witches of Wales in their pointed hats. Queen Mab herself and all her retinue ride round the brim of the magician's hat.

FEMALE NARRATOR. Our laws of space do not apply to this

picture; nor do our laws of being.

None of the plentiful deformities of the swarm of fairy folk astonishes him. He knows each one and welcomes them. And each element in the picture is given the same existential weight. If each ear of corn, each spiked chestnut husk, is rendered with a naturalist's fidelity, so are the spread, fluttering wings and brilliant garb of the crowd, some of whom are so small they are scarcely visible to the naked eye as they glide behind a clod of earth, secrete themselves beneath a blade of grass . . .

And their eyes are full of indifference; a cruel, fierce regard, a fixed grin on all their tiny faces.

FAIRY FELLER. I hold my axe high in the air—

Squeaks, buzzes.

And I s'all bring it down upon this here hazel-nut, which I propose to split in half with one stroke—

Cheers.

—and so resolve the argument—

DADD. —And so resolve the war within me—

Cheers, applause; which abruptly cease.

MALE NARRATOR. But the axe cannot fall. Nothing can move.

FAIRY FELLER. And here we are, stuck fast for all eternity, waiting for me to strike. Waiting . . .

DADD. . . . waiting . . . in the rock and castle of seclusion . . .

FAIRY FELLER. And he's too scared of what he did to let on he knows my secret. That the blow I am about to strike, which he prevents me from, is the very blow he struck hisself!

DADD. Osiris defend me!

DOCTOR. Calm yourself, Mr Dadd. Calm yourself; music . . .why don't you play a little?

Country fiddle plays.

CRAZY JANE. So then he'd play the old fiddle the doctor gave him,

by the hour, see, all the good old tunes such as 'Over the hills and
far away' and 'The Devil among the tailors'. And the music so
took him out of hisself that he don't even notice a poor, mad girl
who'd like her picture made for her . . .

(*Persuasive.*) Oh, Mr Dadd, won't you paint the portrait of
poor Crazy Jane?

Fade fiddle.

MALE NARRATOR. **Sketch of an idea for Crazy Jane**, 1855. Watercolour.

CRAZY JANE. And since there was not one of the female kind
within those walls, Mr Dadd was forced to have a poor, distracted
young man stand in for my body, he wrapped the lad in rags, with
straw, feathers and little flowers such as daisies and vines of
morning glory in my hair. And yet Mr Dadd caught the look of me
to a T, for all that, especially about the eyes, my tragic eyes, you
might say. And from his memory he recalled a lovely background
to my plight, a ruined castle, trees, and, flying across the sky,
crows . . .

Very soft country fiddle; crows.

Yet, see, how they still be English watercolour crows, not the
same crows at all that brought such raucous terror to Crazy
Vincent's canvasses . . .

OBERON.
        Death and affliction, even hell itself,
        She turns to favour and to prettiness.

CRAZY JANE. (*Laughs.*) Mr Dadd? Still playing your old fiddle?

Fiddle louder.

So, hour by hour and year by year, he plays his fiddle, the songs his
nursey sang him long ago, whilst around him we pace out our
shuttered lives from hour to hour, time measured by mealtimes,
by sleeps, by paroxysm . . .

Fiddle fades.

Sketch of an idea for Crazy Jane.
by Richard Dadd. Bethlehem Hospital London ....
September 6th 1855

CRAZY JANE

Sketch to illustrate the Passions
Murder. Cain murders Abel.
by Richard Dadd. Oct 24 1854
Bethlehem Hospital London.

SKETCH TO ILLUSTRATE THE PASSIONS. MURDER

MALE NARRATOR. Dadd's delusion remained fixed and immovable, his behaviour unpredictable. When, in 1864, all the criminal patients of Bethlem were sent to the newly opened asylum at Broadmoor, in Berkshire, Dadd went with them, by train. There was never any possibility of his release; yet, as long as no mention was made of those subjects to which his obsessions were sensitive, his doctors described him as a charming companion. In old age, he took on a benign appearance, with a flowing white beard. The doctors liked him, encouraged him, he painted their portraits, was even allowed to paint frescoes on the walls of their private homes.

DOCTOR. Why, Mr Dadd, very fine; a charming figure of the goddess, Flora, bearing fruit and flowers . . . a veritable harvest festival of fruit and flowers! It's good to see you so busy, so absorbed . . .

Rustling of papers; now he sounds as if he were writing a report.

And yet my sympathetic scrutiny can find very few clues as to the exact nature of his . . . illness . . . in those of his paintings I have seen, that are all the evidence he ever submitted to the world as to the exact state of his inner life. He would settle for a while with those notebooks he retained, still, from that unfortunate journey forty years before and then commit to watercolour or to canvas some Arab or Greek scene, as if his memory were stuck fast at the point before his delusion took hold of him. And the sea, he retained a great affection for painting seascapes; and he had painted, I remember, a series of little moral sketches in his last years at Bethlem, scenes to illustrate the passions, he called them . . . such as Avarice, and Melancholy, and Ambition . . . My colleagues studied his watercolour **Murder** for a long time; it shows, I recall, a wild man, dressed in the skins of beasts, with a great club in his hand with which he has just struck down a similar rough fellow . . . no clue, there. As to the visible documentation of the imaginative experience of a man who had—ahem—committed the patricidal crime of Oedipus, it must be admitted that the paintings of Dadd's madness are curiously . . . unsatisfactory. My Viennese colleague, who took such an interest in that kind of thing did not set up in practice until the spring of the very year that poor Dadd died, in 1886 . . . now, *he* might have been able to extract all manner of meaning from Dadd's pictures; and yet little in them seems, to me, to illuminate his condition, or, indeed, ours . . . for are we not, all of us, residents in the castle of seclusion . . . of the anguished self . . .

Pushes papers aside.

But these are the preoccupations of your century, not of my century! And Dadd, as a madman, had the self-confidence of his period, after all; was he not born of the Age of Assertion?

What would have impressed you most about the poor old boy in his latter years was, what a nice old buffer he was. Prematurely old, of course; institutionalised personality and so forth and quite convinced about this unpleasant Osiris business, wouldn't budge an inch on that. After all, he *had* to believe that or else he'd have realised what it was that he had done, wouldn't he?

FEMALE NARRATOR. The axe never falls, the blow is never struck; self-knowledge, self-realisation remains imminent, never accomplished, the fairies remain fairies, they symbolise nothing . . . even the god whom he invented is not made manifest in his painting.

DOCTOR. But nothing *mad* about his paintings, not at all. Not like some of that damn French stuff you see around nowadays . . . He'd just gone on painting very much the same sort of thing inside Bedlam as he would have painted outside it, d'you see. Business as usual. Just, the perspective went a bit wonky and all the people in the pictures greet you with an uncommonly disconcerting fixed stare . . . And after we all moved to Broadmoor, there was so much to keep him occupied—lantern slides, he painted lantern slides for lectures; and Christmas decorations; and, oh yes, there was a little theatre, where they'd put on plays and shows, don't you know, and he painted a backdrop for that. And some murals. Very nice, little children dancing, that sort of thing. I suppose you could say that the old chap got on with his career as though nothing much had happened.

Dadd sobs; sobbing rises, fades.

What's that? Repression?

FEMALE NARRATOR. The icy calm of absolute repression, the striving both to justify the actions of the self and at the same time to obliterate the actions of the self—

DOCTOR. (*Bored; dismissing the whole subject.*) Well, wasn't he the product of the most repressed society in the history of the world?

MALE NARRATOR. (*Cool.*) The tragic circumstances of Dadd's life were at length terminated by consumption, in Broadmoor, on 8th January 1886.

FEMALE NARRATOR. 'I am truly thankful to know him at rest, it is less grief to me than it was to think of him in the changed condition in which he has lived for many years past, his life has been to me a living death . . . ' Yours faithfully, Mary Anne Dadd, sister of the unfortunate . . .

Fade in to Oberon, coming to the end of his lecture.

OBERON. The quaint pornography of never-never-land; the infection of the mystic East, as fatal to his spirit as the germ of Asiatic cholera was to the flesh of the inhabitants of the foetid cities of the period; the terrible glamour of parricide, a crime which struck at the very root of the patriarchal order of his time which Dadd yet committed, as it were, in absentia, as if even the consciousness of his actions were denied to him. I submit, therefore, that Dadd, rather than an afflicted poetic genius, contrived in some measure, in spite of or, perhaps, because of, his absolute seclusion from it, to capture the essential spirit of his age. For, you creatures of the dream yourselves, could one of you deny that Dadd was himself, in person, the dream's revenge?

Thank you.

Applause; fading into reprise of 'Come unto these Yellow Sands'.

THE COMPANY
OF WOLVES

Fade in cold wind. From the distance we hear the sound of a wolf's cry. It is answered by another then another and another . . . A gust of wind blows the cries away.

ANNOUNCER. 'The Company of Wolves'.

Bring up wind and cross to crackling of log fire centre. Ticking of grandfather clock left centre. Click of knitting needles left. Wide spread.

GRANNY. *(Far left.)* Knit one, purl one, knit two together . . .

RED RIDING HOOD. *(Far right.)* What are you knitting, Granny?

GRANNY. Making some lucky little girl a present.

RED RIDING HOOD. What lucky little girl, Granny?

GRANNY. Lor' love you, my darling, who else would I be knitting a lovely woolly shawl for, if it wasn't for Granny's own pet . . . knit one, purl one . . . a nice shawl to keep her snug, so Granny's darling girl can wrap up warm and cosy, trot through the wood to visit her old grandmother when the winter winds blow and we shall have snow . . . look what a nice red colour the wool is, eh? Red to match baby's rosy cheeks!

RED RIDING HOOD. Quite a bloody red. Quite bloody.

GRANNY. Don't think of nasty things, think of *nice* things. Cosy shawl for Granny's precious girl. Who's Granny's precious girl?

RED RIDING HOOD. *I'm* Granny's precious girl!

GRANNY. And I chose a nice, bright red because you need a bit of colour to cheer you up in winter, in the bleak midwinter . . . knit one, purl one . . . when the snow comes . . .

Fade down domestic noise and overlay with wind.

NARRATOR. *(Close. Centre.)* It is a northern country; a late, brief spring, a cool summer and then the cold sets in again. Cold, tempest, wild beasts in the forests, under the vaulted branches, where it is always dark. When the snow comes, it precipitates in this inhospitable terrain a trance of being, an extended dream that lurches, now and then, into nightmare. The deer, departed to the southern slopes, the cattle all locked up in the byre, now is the time the wild beasts come out, now is the savage time of the year, nothing left for the wolves to eat . . .

Fade up domestic noise, knitting needles etc.

GRANNY. When the snow comes . . . red for danger when the wolves come . . .

Clock, fire, knitting needles all as if blown away by a sudden fierce gust of wind from right to left.

GRANNY & RED RIDING HOOD. (*Flustered.*) Oh! Ah!

We are left with strong wind. Long, low howl right centre back.

GRANNY. (*Distant left.*) Lawks a mercy! The wolves are running!

Peak wind slightly.

NARRATOR. Now is the season of the wolf, the low part of the year when the sun has barely the strength to heave himself up over the horizon. In these days the dire wolf travels in the crepuscular hours—

Wind.

WEREWOLF. (*Back centre. Howls.*)
  I pull my pelt around me and go hunting.
  I can be grey as a cloud or I can be tawny.
  At twilight I roam to tear up the world with my huge claws.
  At twilight I roam to devour the world with my cleaving teeth.
  At twilight I travel with eyes in the back of my head.
  My howl deranges the soo-oul.

Wolf howl. Bring up wind; howling of many wolves from distance.

RED RIDING HOOD. (*Far left, excited.*) What'll we do, Granny? What shall we do?

GRANNY. (*Crossing from far left to right.*) Shut the shutters! Bar the door! Throw more logs on the fire! Make a great blaze! Keep the wolves outside!

As she crosses from left to right so the domestic sounds of fire and clock ticking spread to the right with her and the wind and howling pans right. At the end of the speech she slams shutter shut, right, and this cuts the wind and wolves. Fire rises; clock rises.

(*Returning to left.*) Fear and flee the wolf, my little one.

Knitting resumes.

Purl one . . . knit two together . . . You are always in danger in the forest, where no people are. Oh, my sweet grandchild, whatever you do in the winter weather, never stray from the path through the forest or—

RED RIDING HOOD. (*By Granny.*) What will happen to me, then, Granny?

GRANNY. You'll be lost, instantly, and the wolves will find you! And always be home by nightfall or the wolves will . . .

RED RIDING HOOD. What will they do if they catch me?

GRANNY. Why . . . gobble you up!

Making a game of it, she growls at Red Riding Hood, who giggles delightedly.

Gobble, gobble, gobble . . .

RED RIDING HOOD. (*Running to right.*) Stop it, Granny, you're tickling!

GRANNY. Grrr!

Granny's growls get closer and more menacing. Take down background as the growls crossfade to rending sounds. A piercing scream cuts rending sounds and we are left with cold wind.

NARRATOR. (*Close. Centre.*) After dark comes, they come, they cluster round the forest path, they track your smell of meat as you go through the wood unwisely late. They are like wraiths, like shadows, grey members of a congregation of the damned . . . the beasts of blood and darkness . . . carnivore incarnate, the eternal predator, the perpetual hunger of the dark wood that encompasses the lighted cottage in the clearing, the village trustfully sheltering in the valley . . .

Behind first sentence of following speech lose wind and bring up domestic background:

RED RIDING HOOD. (*Right.*) But I'm not scared of anything. My daddy gave me a big knife—see. Don't I know how to use it? Didn't I see my daddy stick the pig? There's nothing in the wood can harm *me*.

GRANNY. When it gets cold enough, the beasts grow impudent, often I've jumped half out of my skin to see his questing snout under the door and there was a woman once bitten in our village in her own kitchen, as she was straining the macaroni.

RED RIDING HOOD. Straining the macaroni?

GRANNY. Bit in the foot. Purl one, knit one. But the worst thing of all, my dearie, is—some wolves are hairy on the *inside*.

RED RIDING HOOD. What, like a sheepskin jacket? How can *that* be, Granny?

GRANNY. When he be not a natural wolf, my dearie, no wolf at all . . . knit two together.
    Near here, just up the valley, when my own granny was alive, bless her soul, there was a wolf, once, in the winter-time, come savaging the sheep and goats. Oh, such a terror as he was! What massacres he made among the flocks!

Take down fire. Fade up distant baying, baaing, bleating, commotion as from fireplace centre, which through the following sequence becomes a stage for the various backgrounds and action as described by Granny. Fade down to be replaced by fire.

And then this wolf got a taste for man flesh . . .

Fade in geriatric rendition of a hymn: 'All creatures that on earth do dwell . . . '

It ate up a mad old man that used to live in a hut halfway up the mountain and sing to Jesus all day long, innocent as a lamb, he was . . .

Hymn broken off by slavering, chewing.

Once a wolf's tasted human flesh, then nothing else will do.

Fade chewing.

When he'd digested the poor old man, just a few days after, the wolf pounced on a poor little girl, couldn't resist her . . .

Faint girlish scream.

She so white, so tender, a little girl just as old as you are . . .

RED RIDING HOOD. (*Getting close. Far right.*) Twelve. Going on thirteen, thirteen going on fourteen . . . not such a little girl, for all that you baby me, Granny. Thirteen going on fourteen, the hinge of your life, when you are neither one thing nor the other, nor child nor woman, some magic, inbetween thing, an egg that holds its own future in it.

An egg not yet cracked against the cup.

I am the very magic space that I contain. I stand and move within an invisible pentacle, untouched, invincible, immaculate. Like snow. Waiting. The clock inside me, that will strike once a month, not yet . . . wound . . . up . . . .

I don't bleed. I can't bleed.

I don't know the meaning of the word, fear. Fear?

GRANNY. Just your age or a year or so older and she—

Bleating of disturbed sheep, centre back.

was looking after the sheep on the high pasture but she set up such a commotion

Bleating; barking of dogs; girl shouting centre back, men's voices centre back.

that the shepherds came running with their dogs and rifles—

Shouting; barking; shots centre back.

but this old wolf was cunning and soon gave them the slip, off into the woods he went.

Shots etc. Fade.

Fire, clock, knitting, continued:

RED RIDING HOOD. So what happened to the poor wolf, then?

GRANNY. Knit one, purl one . . . I was just coming to that. They sent to the town for a man whose trade was putting down such vermin, famous for it, he was.

Fire effects up.

Fade in digging. Exterior acoustic from fireplace and spread to cover stereo picture. Fade domestic noises.

And this hunter dug—

HUNTER. (*Centre. Close.*)—a pit, with steep sides. A deep pit. A wolf-trap. And in this pit I stuck a sharpened stake and tied to this stake by a string around its left leg a fine—

Quacking, fluttering of wings.

(*With fluttering of wings.*) Now, you just stop that flapping and hold still! (*Close.*) It dearly grieved me, I can tell you, to give such a fat duck to the wolf when I could have roasted it up for meself but there's no better bait in all the world for a wolf than a duck.

Rustles etc. moving left.

So I popped it down the pit and then I covered the pit with branches and settled down in the undergrowth, downwind so he couldn't get a sniff of me, and bided my time . . .

Last rebellious quack. Pause. Rustling from right.

(*Mid left and back—whispering.*) Here he comes . . . what a size! Near as big as I am and how his eyes do shine . . .

Quacking from pit mid right. Crashing sound of branches giving way. Barking of wolf.

GRANNY. And into the trap went the silly wolf.

Animal shriek.

HUNTER. (*Centre.*) So I jumps down and slits—

Throat slitting from pit and grunts from hunter.

his throat, quick as a wink. And commenced to lop off his paws, for I had a fancy to mount this brute's great pads, d'you see, to decorate my mantle, along with the boar's head and the moose head and the great carp my uncle caught ten winters ago that he had stuffed (*Thwack; dull thud.*) . . . but only the one paw did I chop off because, so help me, as I stand here—

(*From pit.*) Mother Mary and all the saints in heaven protect me!

GRANNY. (*Far left.*) Upon the ground the hunter saw there fall no paw at all but—

HUNTER. (*From pit.*) A hand! A man's hand!

Wind faded out:

NARRATOR. (*Centre. Close.*) The desperate claws retract, refine themselves as if attacked by an invisible emery board, until suddenly they become fingernails and could never have been anything but fingernails, or so it would seem. The leather pads soften and shrink until you could take fingerprints from them, until they have turned into fingertips. The clubbed tendons stretch, the foreshortened phalanges extend and flesh out, the bristling hair sinks backwards into the skin without leaving a trace of stubble behind it.

Clock and fire back.

WEREWOLF. (*Approaching from mid right to Red Riding Hood.*)

RED RIDING HOOD. Ooh . . .

WEREWOLF. Now my skin is the same kind of skin as your skin, little sister. There! my hand . . . won't you take hold of my hand?

RED RIDING HOOD. (*Gasps.*)

WEREWOLF. See . . . it's just the same as any other hand, only perhaps a little larger . . . didn't you see the enormous prints I left in the snow?

RED RIDING HOOD. (*Close. Far right.*) Once, one winter when I was little, my father took me out into the wood and we found the track of a wolf, prints as big as dinner-plates, and my father took a good grip of his rifle and peered around but I put my little foot into the print, to match it for size, and I felt all the warmth that lies under the snow swallow me up . . .

GRANNY. (*Far left.*) And now no wolf at all lay before the hunter but the bloody trunk of—

HUNTER. (*Centre.*) So I may never touch another drop, it was a man, with his throat cut and handless, bleeding, dying . . .

NARRATOR. Dead.

Bring up and fade domestic background.

RED RIDING HOOD. (*Thoughtful.*) But I would be sorry for the poor thing, whatever it was, man or beast or some benighted 'twixt and 'tween thing, trapped by a mean trick and finished off without its supper . . .

GRANNY. Knit two together. And worse than that has happened with these vile, unnatural creatures . . . when I was a young thing, about your age, there was a woman in our village married a man who vanished clean away on his wedding night.

Fiddle music: 'The Hunting Boys'.

Rise subdued babble of voices, fiddle music, sound of party from centre back. Fade during following speech but do not replace with domestic sounds.

They made up the bed with new sheets and laid the bride down on it and left them alone together but then the groom said . . .

WEREWOLF. (*From centre back approaching and moving left.*) (*Laughs, embarrassed.*) But, ahem, first of all, before I do join you between the covers, it just so happens, my bonnie, how I must slip outside to answer the call of nature.

BRIDE. (*Mid right.*) Why can't 'ee piss in the pot provided, my love?

WEREWOLF. What, on our wedding night, my dear? In the name of decency . . .

Door slams left.

GRANNY. So she waited . . .

BRIDE. And didn't he look a lovely man, as he stood there in front of the altar and I come down the aisle in my white frock and he turned his head a bit round to see me . . . (*Yawns.*)

Rustle of sheets.

. . . a lovely man, even if his eyebrows meet . . . and he be altogether on the hairy side . . .

GRANNY. . . . and she waited . . .

BRIDE. (*Dreamily.*) and the first, if he be a boy, we shall call after his daddy, but, if she be a girl, why, we'll name her for me mam . . . (*Yawns again.*) . . .

GRANNY. . . . and she waited some more, until she thinks—

BRIDE. . . . surely . . . he's been gone a long time?

Pause; faint wind; howl left.

(*Sitting up in bed—alert.*) God save us all!

NARRATOR. That long-drawn, wavering howl that has, for all its fearful resonances, some inherent sadness in it, as if the beasts would love to be less beastly if only they knew how and never cease, in some wordless, devastating sense, to mourn their own condition.

There is a vast melancholy in the canticles of the wolves, melancholy infinite as the forest, endless as these long nights of winter and yet that ghastly sadness, that mourning for their own, irremediable appetites, can never move the heart, for not one phrase in it hints at the possibility of redemption . . .

Howl of several wolves off left.

Grace could not come to the wolf from its own despair, only through some external mediator . . .

Fade wolves.

BRIDE. (*Close. Right centre.*) When the rumpus died down a bit and I judged it safe to venture into the farmyard, I got down the lantern and searched among the outhouses all in my nightie as I was and that distressed! Oh, weeping and wailing, I was, to think the wolves had eaten up my bridegroom and left nothing behind to bury. For not a gnawed bone nor hank of hair, even, or yet a rag of his wedding suit did I find, but, in the snow, many huge pawprints, as if the beastly things had been having themselves a bit of a dance. A dance!

Sobs; blows nose; recovers.

So then I reckons how he is good and done for so I dried my eyes and went out and found myself another husband not too shy to piss under his own roof and the first boy we named for his father but he would insist the girl be called after me. My bouncing babies, merry as grigs, first they crawl, then they toddle, then they walk, then they run . . . time flies . . . years after, oh, years after, it was one winter's night, one freezing night when the moonlight looks like it could cut you . . . my husband out in the byre tending the cattle, meself in the kitchen with the bairns . . . I just ladling the soup . . . just before Christmas, it was, when nighttime lasts longer than daytime . . .

NARRATOR. It is the season of the solstice, the hinge of the year, the time when things don't fit well together, when the door of the year is sufficiently ajar to let all kinds of beings that have no proper place in the world slip through.

BRIDE. . . . one snowy, moony night . . .

GRANNY. . . . her first good man came home again.

Thump on door, left.

RED RIDING HOOD. (*Far right.*) He hadn't forgotten her, then. He came home for Christmas.

Thump on door repeated.

WEREWOLF. (*Off left.*) Lift up the latch and let me in!

Latch clicks; indrawn breath from bride by door.

BRIDE. (*Right centre. Close.*) I knew him the minute I laid eyes on him, though now he was in rags and his hair grown so, not seen a comb for years, down to his backside, alive with lice, and hell-fire . . . yes! hell-fire darting in his look.

WEREWOLF. (*Entering.*) Here I am again, missus! (*Shuts door.*) Fetch me my bowl of cabbage and be quick about it!

BRIDE. (*Right. Back.*) There's changes made in this house, you villain! You been away too long to have a claim on me!

LITTLE GIRL. (*Off centre.*) Mama!

WEREWOLF. Who's this wee tender morsel?

LITTLE BOY. (*Off centre.*) Mama, mama, what big eyes he has . . .

WEREWOLF. What's this? Cubs? Has this wench been playing among the blankets while her lawful wedded husband's out of the way? You bastards, you by-blows—

Children shriek.

CHILDREN. Mama! Save us!

BRIDE. Don't you dare lay a finger—

WEREWOLF. I wish I were a wolf again, to teach this whore a lesson.

Sounds of clothes being torn off.

BRIDE. (*Close. Right centre.*) And then, he flinging off his coat, his shirt, his boots, his trousers . . . a wolf . . . he instantly . . . became.

Pandemonium; barking; screaming; pots breaking; fire-irons falling.

But my rightful husband, hearing this commotion—

Door opens left.

and hastening in . . .

HUSBAND. What's up then?

BRIDE. . . . seized the axe we used to chop up firewood—

Thwack; scream; groan; thud; silence.

HUSBAND. (*Back. Centre left.*) That's fixed him.

BRIDE. So the father of my children made an end of my . . . visitor . . . then and there, such a mess he made, blood and guts all over the kitchen floor, with one blow struck off its head, and the torso twitched a bit, but then—

BOY. Mama, its fur—

GIRL. Its fur is all melting away—

BRIDE. And, indeed, its hairy pelt fell off like snow off a roof in February, when the thaw comes, and you could see how he was nothing but an ordinary man, underneath, and the years since I'd last seen him had scarcely touched him . . . and his head, that had rolled onto the hearth and come to rest just by the kettle, the furry head with the sharp ears and brindled muzzle and dreadful, crushing jaw . . . why, then it turned back into *his* head, and there was my old sweetheart's face . . . with that self-same smile on it that he'd given me long ago, when we were young, when I walked down the aisle towards him, me in my white lace dress, and he'd turned round to look at me, given me a bit of a smile, as if to say, courage, lass . . . and I never did care that his eyebrows met . . . so now I couldn't forbear to . . .

Bride weeps. Centre right back.

HUSBAND. Is this the thanks I get for butchering the beast? You harlot, I'll fairly larrup you, I will—take that—

Thump; cry; renewed weeping; fade out weeping.

Fade in domestic noise of Granny's kitchen: clock; fire; knitting.

GRANNY. Knit two together . . . now. I'm just ready to cast off, see how it's done? Then your shawl'll be ready to slip round your little shoulders . . .

Pause.

RED RIDING HOOD. How.

GRANNY. How?

RED RIDING HOOD. Do they let their insides come outside?

GRANNY. It is the devil's reward for long service! For they do say there is a salve the devil gives 'em, hands it out at the Sabbath . . .

NARRATOR. Fat of a cat; camphor; aniseed; opium, all mixed together, rubbed well into the skin.

GRANNY. Or they do sup a drink the devil makes—

NARRATOR. An infusion of mandrake, belladonna, henbane, taken in a glass of wine.

GRANNY. Or else they drink from a stream the devil shows 'em and go ravenning off. Or sip the rainwater out of a wolf's pawprint, that is the size of a basin. And some are born so, those that come into the world feet first on St John's Eve and had a wolf for a father . . . and his torso will be a man's but his legs, his privates, those of a wolf . . . and he will have a wolf's heart.

RED RIDING HOOD. A wolf's heart.

GRANNY. Before he can turn into a werewolf, he must always strip stark naked. Peel off all his human concealments, down to the bald, natural buff. If you spy a naked man among the pines, my dearie, you must run as if the devil were after you.

RED RIDING HOOD. A naked man? In *this* weather? He'd have his thingumajigs frozen off, Granny!

She laughs.

GRANNY. Well, just watch out!

But Red Riding Hood continues to laugh. Her laughter fades into sound of wind and storm. Wind and storm peak and fade into country morning sounds—cock-crow, mooing of cows.

MOTHER. (*Left back.*) Just you watch out.

RED RIDING HOOD. (*Right centre. Close.*) I must and will go to Granny's house today. I've set my mind upon it.

MOTHER. Then don't leave the path through the wood—

RED RIDING HOOD. I've got the big, red shawl my granny knitted me, that'll keep me warm, and my mother is packing a basket—

MOTHER. (*Packing basket.*)—oatcakes, butter, cheese—

RED RIDING HOOD. Full of good things for the poor old lady.

MOTHER. . . . a little pot of bramble jelly . . . Oh, you spoilt one, oh, you wilful one! But, if off you must go, on such a cold winter's day, the shortest day of all the year, then be sure to keep to the path through the wood and don't—

RED RIDING HOOD. —stay out—

MOTHER. —after nightfall—

RED RIDING HOOD. —or else—

MOTHER. —the wolves—

RED RIDING HOOD. —will gobble me up.

Red Riding Hood laughs.

MOTHER. If your daddy were here, he'd never let you—

RED RIDING HOOD. But he's out in the forest, picking up sticks.

MOTHER. (*Sighs—aside to audience.*) She being the youngest and, yes, the prettiest, our little bud, our blossom, I can deny her nothing. And she, she's such a high opinion of herself she thinks the snow'll forebear to fall upon her . . .

RED RIDING HOOD. And here I've got my daddy's knife . . . don't I know how to stick the pigs with it?
I shall and will go to Granny's house today.

MOTHER. I'll just slip a bottle of ardent spirits into your basket, to keep the old lady's bones warm . . .

Clink.

MOTHER. (*Going off left.*) . . . and don't stray off the path for a minute and don't let the sun go down with you still outdoors—

Door slams left. Fade up birdsong. Woodland noises.

RED RIDING HOOD. (*Right centre.*) If it were summer, I should pick the flowers and chase the butterflies but now it is winter, only last night's snow on the bare boughs, no reason to dawdle . . . how my breath smokes!

Robin sings.

Well! here's the robin, the friend of man in his bloody waistcoat, perched on a stump to wish me good morning.

Fade robin; footsteps on rustic path.

And if I walk quiet as I can, then I may spy Reynard the Fox taking home a hen out of my daddy's run so his family can have some dinner . . .

Raucous caw.

A raven . . . why, Reynard the Fox has been out early, this morning; here's the blood of some poor slaughtered bunny on the snow, the horrid raven pecking it . . . shoo, you cannibal, shoo!

Caw; flapping of wings; distant howl.

What's that?

Rustle of undergrowth; an arrival.

WEREWOLF. (*Right.*) Oh, please, young lady, put away that knife! How fierce you look! I never intended to startle you, I would have thought there was nobody in all the wood but me.

RED RIDING HOOD. Well, well, well . . . who's this fine young man, sprung up out of nowhere . . .

GRANNY (*on echo*). (*Repeated from first time.*) If you spy a naked man in the forest, run as if the devil were after you . . .

RED RIDING HOOD. But this one's got all his clothes on, Granny! Such nice clothes, too . . . lovely bit of tweed, that jacket, with the leather patches on the elbows. And a felt hat with a feather in the band. And nice whipcord breeches, and such a shine on his leather boots! It took a gentleman's gentleman to give *this* gentleman's boots that shine. Out after game, he must be out after game . . . doesn't he have his rifle over his shoulder?

WEREWOLF. Here I am, a jolly huntsman.

RED RIDING HOOD. So he makes me a little bow, polite as can be, and—

WEREWOLF. Allow me.

Takes basket.

RED RIDING HOOD. What lovely manners, taking the heavy old basket off me to carry himself. Not like those rude clowns in the village who don't know how to treat a lady, let a girl hump the potato sacks all by herself—oh, my knife! I put my knife in the basket!

WEREWOLF. My rifle will protect us both, young lady. You have nothing to fear when you are with me. Permit me—

Footsteps in undergrowth.

RED RIDING HOOD. So this fine young gentleman takes my arm and off we go together, as if we were out for a ramble, and soon we're chattering away together as if we'd sucked on the same nipple . . .

Fade in conversation, burst of laughter. The following four speeches are all faded in/out but background remains constant.

RED RIDING HOOD. —taking a few bits of this and that to my old granny, sir, seeing as she is bedridden—

WEREWOLF. —parted company with my friends in order to bang away by myself and now making for the village—

RED RIDING HOOD. —make haste and speed for the day darkens early, this time of year—

WEREWOLF. —hoping to find some friendly hostelry, a bite to eat, a drink—

RED RIDING HOOD. (*Clean in.*) Should you escort me as far as my granny's house, sir, I'm sure my granny would gladly give you a cup of tea, or maybe something a bit stronger, seeing as how we slipped a bottle of brandy in with the butter and cheese.

WEREWOLF. Delighted. Delighted.

RED RIDING HOOD. (*Close centre left.*) And me all of a flutter, poor, simple girl that I am. For he is such a *handsome* young fellow, for all his eyebrows do grow close together . . .

WEREWOLF. (*Close centre right.*) Fifteen going on sixteen, the tenderest age. Under that red shawl, how white her skin must be, as white as breast of chicken, succulent as loin of pork . . .
    Little miss, pretty miss, see what I have in my pocket!

RED RIDING HOOD. Now, this young man had the most remarkable object in his pocket, which he brought forth to show to me. At first I thought it was perhaps some kind of a pocket watch, for it was round and swung on a chain. But *tick* it did not, and then it came to me how it might be a locket with a picture of his sweetheart inside, which made me squint a bit, until he said—

WEREWOLF. This is what we call a compass.

RED RIDING HOOD. It had a round face, much like a clock, but no numbers on it and only the one hand, that moved around in a wavering manner. Wavering as if it were looking for something.

WEREWOLF. Looking for the north.

RED RIDING HOOD. And he told me how this compass had helped him find his way through the trackless forest, because the needle always pointed to the north with perfect accuracy—

WEREWOLF. So, you see, I can never lose my way! I'm always at home in the forest.

RED RIDING HOOD. But I did not believe him. I knew I should never leave the way on the path through the wood or else I should be lost instantly.

WEREWOLF. (*Laughs close.*) Why, I can guarantee you, if I plunge off this winding path directly into the wood, now, at this moment, and find my way by the compass, I will arrive at your grandmother's house a good quarter of an hour before you do. I promise you!

RED RIDING HOOD. I shan't leave the path; I won't leave the path.

WEREWOLF. Then . . . you stay on the path and I'll go through the

wood and we'll see who gets to your granny's house first. Is it a
wager? Shall we make a little bet on it?

RED RIDING HOOD. You get there how you like; I'll get there how I
like.

WEREWOLF. What will you give me if I get there before you?

Pause.

RED RIDING HOOD. (*Disingenuous.*) What would you like me to
give you?

Pause.

WEREWOLF. A kiss. (*Close.*) How she's blushing, like blood
leaking into the snow . . .

Owl hoots—ominous noises.

RED RIDING HOOD. Look how dark it's getting! Why, I do believe
we'll have more snow—

WEREWOLF. A kiss?

RED RIDING HOOD. (*Bursts out laughing.*) You're on—

Swish—the werewolf vanishes into the wood.

Here, hold on—you've taken my basket with you! And my knife,
you've taken my knife!

Undergrowth rustles at distance.

Oh, never mind it, I'll soon catch up with him . . . (*Giggles.*) What
an adventure, though! Indeed . . . for fear of catching up with him
too soon . . . I'll take my time, I will, over this last half mile to
Granny's house, although the snow is coming on . . .

Fade her. Bring up wind. Fade in footsteps in undergrowth.

WEREWOLF. (*Hums to himself the seduction song from 'Don
Giovanni'.*)

NARRATOR. Towards the fringes of the forest, nestling in a clearing, a cottage whose ruddy windows beamed with cheerful light
as if, in the approaching dark and the whirling beginnings of the

snow, that house contained all the human warmth in the world.

Towards the cottage door the huntsman now purposefully directed his footsteps.

Crossfade background to fire crackling, clock ticking, etc. Rat-a-tap-tap from right.

GRANNY. (*Crossing from left to right.*) Who's that knocking on my door?

WEREWOLF. (*Off—falsetto.*) Only your granddaughter, come all this way to see you on a cold and snowy evening!

Latch lifted. Door, right, opened. A big wind blows through the house, blows away the domestic noises.

NARRATOR. And by his incandescent eyes, she knew at once the nature of her visitor, and, clasping her hands together, she besought—

GRANNY. JesuJosephMarySaintAnneSaintElizabethSaint—

WEREWOLF. Call on all the saints in the calendar to speed hot-foot from heaven to help you, Granny, but it won't do you any good. How can you keep the night out, when it wants so much to come in?

GRANNY. (*Screams.*) (*Far left over her own scream 'as heard before'.*) Before he can become a wolf, the werewolf strips stark naked.

WEREWOLF. (*Undressing.*) . . . good . . . to get out of these silly clothes . . .

GRANNY. Under his clothes, he was the colour of goatcheese, and nipples black as poison berries, and a stripe of hair running down his belly, and so thin, he was, that you could count his ribs . . .

WEREWOLF. . . . but I'm not going to give you any time . . .

NARRATOR. And now, as the old lady quivered with dread before him, she witnessed the unimaginable metamorphosis, the coarse, grey, the tawny, bristling pelt springing out from the bare skin of her visitor . . . great jaw slavering . . . his red eyes, now burning with far greater intensity than the coals in her hearth . . .

GRANNY. . . . and his privates, of a wolf, huge . . . he naked as a stone, but hairy . . . he . . . aaaaaaagh! (*Echo.*)

Fade Granny. Hold wind for a moment. Then fade in logs crackle, clock ticks, mastication and lose wind.

WEREWOLF. (*Right centre.*) Here's a tough old bird, indeed . . . veritable jaw-cracker . . . Not much meat on her, all sinew . . . still, waste not, want not; down the red lane with Granny . . . and isn't dessert trotting through the wood towards me this minute, and she tender as a peach . . . juicy as a wood strawberry . . .

Swallow. Lip-smacking. Belch.

NARRATOR. When he had finished with her, he quickly dressed himself again, until he was just as he had been when he came through the door. He burned the inedible hair in the fireplace—

Whizz of flame.

and wrapped up the bones in the tablecloth.

Faint rattle of bones centre.

WEREWOLF. What, Granny, shaking your old bones at me? Playing a tune on your own xylophone (*Moving left.*) I'll put you under the bed, out of harm's way . . . don't you know I've done for you, Granny?

Rattle of bones thrown under bed, left.

(*As he moves centre.*) Oops! here's my rifle; best hide it up the chimney, lest dessert takes a mind to shoot it off at me . . . why, here's her basket; oatcakes, butter . . . cheese . . . nothing fit for a carnivore to eat . . . hello, brandy! How about a little digestive, Granny?

Pours, drinks.

Here's . . . to your posthumous health! (*Moving left.*) Now . . . settle down in Granny's chair. Best . . . put on . . . the old lady's nightcap, don't want to scare away the little pretty if she peeks through the window to see if her handsome huntsman got here before her. (*Laughs.*)

Settles down; resumes humming air from 'Don Giovanni'.
Clock whirs, strikes half-hour.

Where can she have got to . . .

Rat-a-tap-tap. Right.

(*Falsetto.*) Who's that knocking on my door?

RED RIDING HOOD. (*Off.*) Didn't a young gentleman get here before me, Granny?

WEREWOLF. (*Falsetto, moving to right centre.*) Young gentleman? What young gentleman? I've seen no young gentleman!

RED RIDING HOOD. Oh . . .

WEREWOLF. Lift up the latch and come in, like a dutiful grand-daughter!

Latch lifts, door opens; intensification of domestic noises. Fade slightly.

RED RIDING HOOD. (*Close centre.*) And then, oh, then, how I did want the big knife my father gave me, to do for him—oh, yes, I did. But as for my knife, I could not get it, it being in my basket, my basket being on the table and him standing between me and the table, tall and wild as if all the wild wood was made into a man and it come into the kitchen and his eyes as big as saucers, flaming—

Bring up fire, clock, etc.

What big eyes you have.

WEREWOLF. All the better to see you with, my pretty. You're a sight worth looking at.

RED RIDING HOOD. (*Close centre.*) And there was no trace of my granny anywhere in the kitchen, but for a tuft of white hair caught in an unburned bit of log in the grate, and then I knew I was in danger of death.
    What have you done with my granny?

WEREWOLF. There's nobody here but we two, darling.

RED RIDING HOOD. (*Close.*) Then fear of death over me, I, who had been afraid of nothing, for, though I knew that he had just eaten, yet I know the wolf is always hungry . . .

And I cannot cry for help because we are a good mile from the village.

Single howl outside.

Yet though I am among the wild beasts—

More howling.

I must not be afraid because fear is their meat—

Yet more howling.

and so I must not suffer it.

Fade howling until very soft. She takes a deep breath.

Who has come to sing to us?

WEREWOLF. Those are the voices of my brothers, darling. I love the company of wolves. Look out of the window and you'll see them.

RED RIDING HOOD. (*Moving right.*) How it's snowing! You can't see through the lattice, the pane all caked with snow . . .

WEREWOLF. Open the window . . .

Lattice opens. Peak wind, wolf-chorus. Take down behind.

RED RIDING HOOD. (*Close.*) And on the branches of the apple tree outside my granny's window were perched a fruit of wolves . . . it had become a wolf tree . . . they all staring at me with their big, dumb eyes, eyes with such sorrow in the pupils . . . ten wolves, twenty wolves, more wolves than I could count . . . eyes catching the light from the kitchen and shining like candles . . . each beast pointing its muzzle to the moon and howling fit to break your heart . . .

Lattice slams shut. Cut wind and howling.

It's freezing cold, poor things, no wonder they howl so.

WEREWOLF. (*Caressing.*) Are you cold, too, my darling? Would you like a glass of brandy, to warm you?

RED RIDING HOOD. Oh, it's warm enough, indoors, by the fire.

WEREWOLF. Then take off . . . your shawl.

RED RIDING HOOD. What . . . shall I do with it, now?

WEREWOLF. Burn it, dear one. You won't need it again.

RED RIDING HOOD. (*Close.*) So I stuffed the shawl in the fireplace,
and, seeing the bottle of brandy my mam gave me to give Granny,
I dowsed the fire with it, to make the flames jump up.

   Fire crackles.

WEREWOLF. The light! My eyes!

RED RIDING HOOD. And up the chimney went the red shawl that
my granny knitted me, it catching fire on the way, whoosh! Look!
Like a bird with flamy wings!

WEREWOLF. (*Groans.*)

RED RIDING HOOD. (*Close.*) And, just as if my granny were angry
with me for setting light to her shawl, there came such a rattling of
her old bones . . .

   Staccato rattle from left.

Well . . . I do think, tonight, on such a night, that I should wear
nothing but my skin, for why should I go clothed when the poor
wolves outside do not . . .

   Rattle of bones.

my skirt . . . my blouse . . . one stocking . . . two stockings . . .
onto the fire! What a blaze!

   Rattling. Flames.

RED RIDING HOOD. Oh, hush and be quiet, Granny, while your
granddaughter entertains your visitor!

   Bones give one last, disapproving rattle.

WEREWOLF. (*Whimpers.*)

RED RIDING HOOD. There. See? All my clothes burned up. Oh, sir,
your eyes—they're watering! Are you in pain? Can't you bear the

bright light?

WEREWOLF. (*Sobs and whimpers.*) My eyes . . .

RED RIDING HOOD. Oh, sir, don't turn your head away . . . not from poor girl like me. Or is it the firelight has got into my skin, too?

Do I *blaze*, sir? Am I too bright for you, sir?

WEREWOLF. I can't . . . I can't . . .

RED RIDING HOOD. What is it, sir? Is it that you're having some difficulty about turning into a wolf, sir, because I've had my clothes off first? Is that it?

WEREWOLF. Aren't you frightened of the wolf?

RED RIDING HOOD. Since my fear did me no good, I put it away from me, sir; put it away with my clothes.

Oh, fine gentleman! Fair is fair. If I am to go naked, then you must go naked, too. Let me unbutton that shirt for you . . . Don't struggle, now . . . what does my mammy say, 'Let's skin the rabbit' . . . but *this* rabbit has fur *underneath* his skin . . .

What big arms you have. There . . . put them around me . . . there . . .

WEREWOLF. (*Groans.*)

RED RIDING HOOD. I do believe, since you got here before me, that you owe me a kiss.

What big teeth you have!

WEREWOLF. (*Choking—grabbing at straws.*) All the better . . . to eat you with.

RED RIDING HOOD. Oh, I say!

She goes into peals of laughter.

Well, each to his meat but I am meat for no man! Now I shall burn your clothes, just like I burned my own . . .

WEREWOLF. Not that!

RED RIDING HOOD. Why, anybody would think you were scared of being a good wolf all the time . . .

Flames blaze.

And now I shall see you as the good wolf you are, the honest wolf, the kind wolf.

For to their own, the wolves are tender, are they not? If you were truly a wolf, would you not let me climb up on your back and take me home through the forest.

Bring up fire, wolves and storm outside right.

WEREWOLF. (*Furry voice.*) Outside's not the place to be, tonight, the snow, the freezing blast . . . stay indoors with me, lie down on Granny's bed . . .

RED RIDING HOOD. What, make ourselves cosy?

Bed creaks.

RED RIDING HOOD. There we are . . . lay your head in my lap, there . . .your great, grey, grizzled head . . . let me scratch your lovely ears, you can hear the clouds move, can't you, you can hear the grass grow, such sensitive ears, so quick of hearing . . . and I can see the lice move on your fur, poor beast . . .

Growl.

And shall I pick the lice out, would that be a kindness to you . . .

Appreciative growl. Clock whirs—about to strike. Clock strikes twelve—fade down while it is still striking. Distant wind. Fire.

NARRATOR. Midnight. The blizzard will die down; the door of the solstice stands wide open.

RED RIDING HOOD. (*Yawns.*) She's drowsy, she's sleepy . . . how soft your fur is! Warm!

Clock out.

WEREWOLF. When I was a man, I heard a story that, then, I did not believe because I thought that all the wolves were as I was.

How there was a woman lived on the mountain and she went into labour in winter, in a storm, and bore her little daughter and died of it, nobody by but her husband. He did what he could but when there was no hope for her, he went off to the village to fetch the priest, the snow falling, the wind blowing, and the ice on the river broke under him, he drowned.

When the storm passed off, this woman's mother went out to see after her and found a corpse but no baby, not a trace, so they all thought the wolves had eaten her. And seven years went by, until another hard winter when the wolves came out of the forest, after the goats, and the dead woman's mother saw a creature with long hair, that might have been a little girl, and she running with them. And they found footprints among the pawprints. Footprints.

So they scoured the mountain and found the child in a cave, with an old, grey wolf they shot when it jumped up at them. Then they took the girl back to the village and locked her in a barn, but she howled; how she howled. She howled until she brought every wolf out from all over the forest, dozens of them, hundreds of them, howling in concert as if demented, and the wolves laid siege to the barn and would let nobody near and the girl ran away with them.

And seven years later, the old woman, she was out gathering mushrooms, she saw a grown woman with two pups, kneeling by the river, lapping up water. But when the old woman called out 'My dear one, my pet, come back to me!' off the other one ran to where her friends were waiting.

Are you listening? Are you sleeping?

RED RIDING HOOD. (*Stirs, murmurs wordlessly in her sleep.*)

NARRATOR. The blizzard died down, leaving the woods as randomly covered with snow as if a clumsy cook had knocked the flour bin over them.

Moonlight, snowlight, a confusion of pawprints under the apple tree outside the window.

All silent, all still.

WEREWOLF. She's sleeping, look, her paws twitch, she's dreaming of rabbits . . .

NARRATOR. Sweet and sound she sleeps in Granny's bed, between the paws of the tender wolf.

Fade fire crackling and clock.

VAMPIRELLA

Gently fade in cooing of doves and bring into foreground the song of a lark on interior acoustic.

COUNTESS. (*Over.*) Can a bird sing only the song it knows or can it learn a new song . . .

HERO. . . . said the lovely, lonely, lady vampire, running the elegant scalpel of her fingernail along the bars of the cage in which her pet bird sang.

The sound of the Countess's nails against the bars of the cage. The Countess laughs: and her laugher is picked up by a harp which mirrors her laughter—the lark sings; cut short by the screech of a bat.

Fade in doves cooing as before. The lark sings, the Countess laughs, and her laughter, as before, is repeated by the harp and is then crossfaded to her fingers running along the bars of the birdcage—in the same key.

COUNTESS. (*Over.*) My demented and atrocious ancestors habitually sequested themselves from the light of the sun in solemn, indeed, lugubrious, heavily curtained apartments; each one, man or woman, was a victim of the most terrible passion.

A screech from the bat.

. . . Ah!—scarcely dare to speak its name. Even the meanest fiend in hell shuns the company of my kind. I am compelled to the repetition of their crimes; that is my life. I exist only as a compulsion, a compulsion . . .

COUNT. (*Thoughts microphone.*) In Hungary, in the county of Temesvar, those who fall sick of the fatal lethargy that follows my embraces say that a white spectre follows them, sticking as close to their heels as does a shadow. They track down the dreaded vampire by means of the following ritual. They choose a young boy who is a pure maiden, that is to say, who has not yet known any woman, and set him bareback on a stallion that has not mounted its first mare. The power of these two virgins exists, you understand, only in containment. Like me, like she, they possess the mysterious solitude of ambiguous states . . . they are not linked into the great chain of generation. We are all unnatural. Horse and rider trot towards the village cemetery—

*Bring in exterior acoustic—owls etc. and the clip-clop of a
horse—centre.*

—and go in and out among the gravestones while the peasantry
follow with spades and scythes and crucifixes and wreaths of
garlic. Breathlessly, they creep a little way behind the emissaries of
virginity . . . until—

*During above bring in murmur of villagers which ends on a
gasp.*

BOY. See! He's stopped! He won't budge an inch! (*Steps.*) Here,
here! In this grave, beneath this stone, the vampire lies!

*Shovelling. Clink of spade upon coffin. Creaking: they are
opening the coffin.*

Ah!

The villagers react to what they see.

COUNT. (*Close.*) There the quarry lies, as ruddy in the cheeks as if
I had nodded off to sleep in my shroud. I might have been taking a
little after-dinner nap, replete, pacific . . . The priest takes up a
heavy sword and . . .

Sharp blow. Rapid intonation in Greek.

So they strike off my head and out gushes warm torrents of rich,
red blood, like melted roses.

Gasps. Rapid praying.

BOY. The land is freed from the plague of vampires!

*Cheers and applause. Down behind following and creep in
music.*

COUNT. Endlessly, I attend my own obsequies; softly, enormously, across all my funerals, my fatal shadow rises again . . .

COUNTESS. But love, true love, could free me from this treadmill,
this dreadful wheel of destiny . . .

COUNT. My daughter, the last of the line, through whom I now
project a modest, posthumous existence, believes herself to be a

version of the Flying Dutchman—that she may be made whole by human feeling. That one, fine day, a young virgin will ride up to the castle door and restore her to humanity with a kiss from his pure, pale lips.

The Countess sighs dreadfully which cuts music and drily sobs.

Oh, my little girl, I'd love to see you lie quiet . . .

Fade in exterior acoustic—bicycle wheels on a track.

HERO. (*Thoughts microphone.*) Night and silence. I never guessed, here in the Carpathians, would be no stars. No stars, no moon. I am just a little nervous, although no one is here . . . Is it only a simple twanging of my own nerves that I feel? Yet I am not a timorous man. My colonel assures me I have nerves of steel. But I might almost be prepared to believe this fear no more than a sudden crisis of my own, a revisitation of all the childhood fears of night and silence in my present loneliness, the uncanny dark of this Carpathian tea-time . . . I would be inclined to believe I was so innocently afraid if I did not possess a strange conviction that terror itself was in some sense immanent in these particular rocks and bushes. I've never felt such terror in any other place. The North West Frontier, far more barren, far more inimical . . . damn deserts never scared me so. It is as if terror were the genius loci of the place and only comes out at night. When they told me this morning at the inn I should not stay out beyond the fall of darkness, I did not believe them. But I was not in the least afraid, then.

Owl hoots, long, lonely sound. The bicycle wheels wobble, click against stone. Hero exclaims.

Ah! ah, nothing but a nightbird. The cry of a nightbird momentarily startled me, so that I nearly fell.

Bicycle wheels steady on track.

They say the owl was a baker's daughter . . . not a bird of the best of omens.
(*Brisker, less introspective tone.*) To ride a bicycle is in itself some protection against superstitious fears since the bicycle is the product of pure reason applied to motion. Geometry at the service of man! Give me two spheres and a straight line and I will show you how far

I can take them. Voltaire himself might have invented the bicycle, since it contributes so much to man's well-being and nothing at all to his bane. Bicycling is beneficial to the health. The bicycle emits no harmful fumes and permits only the most decorous speeds. It is not a murderous implement.

Yet, like all the products of enlightened reason, the bicycle has a faint air of eccentricity about it. On two wheels in the Land of the Vampires! A suitable furlough for a member of the English middle classes. My first choice was, the Sahara. But then, I thought, perhaps a more peopled tour would be more fascinating . . .

Nobody is surprised to see me, they guess at once where I come from. The coarse peasants titter a little behind their hands. Le Monsieur Anglais! But they behave with deference; for only a man with an empire on which the sun never sets to support him would ride a bicycle through this phantom-haunted region.

Pause. Bring up bicycle slightly.

A bicycle is a lonely instrument.

Hoot of owl.

To ride a bicycle involves a continuous effort of will and hence it is a moral exercise. A purposive retention of the perpendicular in circumstances, such as the presence of great fear, when the horizontal—lying flat on the ground scrabbling helplessly with one's fingers in the soil in order to dig oneself a hole in which to hide—would seem to be by far the more sensible thing to do.

Now we approach a rustic bridge.

The wheels now rattle as they cross bridge—matching hero's mood.

Something atavistic, something numinous about crossing whirling dark water by no moonlight . . .

COUNT. (*Very softly.*) And when he crossed the bridge, the phantoms came to meet him . . .

Rattle of the bicycle wheels increased.

HERO. I do believe that now I am so frightened that when the front wheels of my bicycle jolt upon that stone—or is it the skull of a wild beast—that skull or stone I see before me in the tremulous light of my headlamp, I will go flying from my saddle and tumble headlong into the stream, since my fear has so overcome my sense or senses that I can no longer retain the vertical in the face of any unexpected obstacle, however small. (*He gives a sudden cry.*)

A crash, a splash, a moan: the bicycle wheels run on. One wheel spins round more and more slowly until at last it stops. Crossfade to running water. Hero moans as he drags himself ashore. Distantly, a babble of rough voices gradually getting louder. The voices speak an improvised language full of Ks and Ts. They come across hero and begin, curiously, inspecting him.

HERO. I say, gently does it! Can nobody speak English? Not one word? I say, where are you taking me?

Kindly, firmly they pick him up, exchanging guttural remarks and occasionally pinching him. Their big boots clatter on the track as they lead him away.

(*Over.*) Well, I daresay I'll find out where they're taking me soon enough. Could do with a rest. I could do with . . . a cup of tea. Quite a nasty fall, really—just a little shaken, I must confess. A good, hot cup of tea, now . . . My God, how English I am! It never ceases to astonish me.

Why have they left my bicycle behind, though? Lying where it fell, among the weeds at the side of the bridge, the dew will rust it . . .

Footsteps now on cobbles.

Ah, a light before us. We must be going towards that light. A light, a homestead in this abandoned and desolate region. Yet that light does not console me, it does not make me think of home and hearth and fireside. It is a sinister and flickering light, like marsh-fire . . . By God, a castle! And flambeaux at the gates; great, whirling bouquets of gas, darting hither and thither on the wind!

Hissing of gas-jets.

COUNT. (*Thoughts microphone.*) . . . a vast, ruined castle, from whose tall black windows came no ray of light and whose broken battlements showed a jagged line . . . like broken teeth. And at my gate I light the visitor a welcome with fireflowers plucked from hell . . .

> *Dog snarls: a mournful clanging of a bell. Gate creaks open, melodramatically.*

HERO. The gatekeeper, a horn lantern in his horny fist; lighting up constellations of cobwebs . . . !

> *Peasants depart, giggling unpleasantly. Door clangs shut. Footsteps on stone floor.*

I am alone. Dear God, I never heard any portal close behind me with such an emphatic clang. How I'm shivering; these wet clothes . . .

GATEKEEPER. (*Says something incomprehensible.*)

HERO. Good evening. (*Hero sits, with a sigh of relief.*) Must be the concierge's private quarters. Quite clean, quite comfortable . . . a bit Spartan . . . guns on the walls. No spik English, eh?

> *Grunt from gatekeeper.*

Well, I daresay we'll get on well enough. My, what a fine fire . . . (*Rubs hands at the crackling blaze.*) Ah, a change of clothes, ready laid out for me . . . why—just my size! A nice piece of worsted, that suit, and a fine silk shirt, monogrammed upon the breast . . . A Cyrillic delta, indeed . . . Ready laid out, as if they were expecting me. And a stout pair of shoes. (*Hero is changing clothes during speech.*) That's better, clean, dry clothes. And judging by the gatekeeper's manoeuvres with that bottle, that glass, I should imagine I'm about to be treated to a little peasant hospitality.

> *Bottle emptying into glass.*

Thanks! (*Drinks: coughs.*) Some kind of vodka, very strong . . . warming. I'd certainly not say no to another.

> *Another glass is poured. Footsteps and effects in background.*

Now what are you up to! Ah, getting me some black bread, is it? Black bread and cheese. I could do with a bite, I must say. I suppose I'll be lodging here for the night. Only one bed . . .

perhaps I'll doss down on the floor, with the dog. Eh, boy?

Dog barks excitedly.

COUNT. (*Thoughts microphone.*) Down, boy, down!

Dog whimpers.

HERO. Backing away from me, now? Oh, come, the English have a traditional affinity for dogs . . . but not, perhaps, for such dogs as you, you great, slavering, fanged monster! Yes, wild dog, indeed.

COUNT. (*Thoughts microphone.*) Red-eyed devil's whelp, many a witless ancient died a ghastly death at the hands of the inquisition for petting in her bosom such a familiar as you . . . if you are a good dog and don't bite the carpet or foul the floor, my daughter will throw you a juicy bone, a femur with some scraps of flesh still on it, perhaps.

Door creaks open.

HERO. (*To himself.*) What have we here, what apparition in black velvet. A valet, by his obsequiousness, the chatelaine's valet? He's gesturing towards me. Why, he's dumb! . . . (*Aloud.*) Taking me off somewhere, are you? Off to meet the king of the castle? No need to clasp my wrist so tight . . . I'll come quietly.

Footsteps echo on stone floor.

COUNT. (*Ghostly chuckle disappearing into echoes.*)

Crossfade to Mrs Beane. Fire crackling in background.

MRS BEANE. (*Baleful, humorous—off microphone.*)
        Fee, fi, fo, fum.
        I smell the blood of an Englishman.

Och, it's only my pawky Scots humour that preserves my sanity!

COUNTESS. I am the lady of the castle. My name is exile. My name is anguish. My name is longing. Far, far from the world on the windy crests of the mountain, I am kept in absolute seclusion, my time passes in an endless revery, a perpetual swooning. I am both the Sleeping Beauty and the enchanted castle; the princess drowses in the castle of her flesh.

MRS BEANE. Hush, hush my dearie, don't distress yourself.

Ripple of larksong.

COUNTESS. (*Shivers.*) Cold, so cold, Mrs Beane . . . the wind creeps in through the cracks in the old stone and the fire never warms me.

MRS BEANE. (*To a child.*) Now, you just stop feeling sorry for yourself and eat up your egg. Look, I've cut up your bread and butter into soldiers for you . . .

COUNTESS. (*As child.*) Shall I eat up the nice soldiers?

MRS BEANE. Like a good girl, now . . . och, your hands are like ice!

COUNTESS. Since a child, so cold. Always cold. I should like to go to a land of perpetual summer and let the petals of a flowering tree fall upon my face as I lie in the warm shade and sleep without the fever of this eternal shivering. But could even Italian summers warm me, when not all the fires of Hell might do so—

MRS BEANE. (*Angry.*) Countess! Now, just you stop your whining!

COUNTESS. (*Almost sulky.*) Shunned by fiends . . .

COUNT. (*Thoughts microphone.*) Does my beautiful daughter sense her father's posthumous presence or is she indeed a portion of myself . . .

Door opens, off.

HERO. (*Thoughts microphone.*) In the dark, luxurious room, I made out two figures beside the little fire, a craggy dame with pepper and salt hair dragged back in an austere bun, upright as a standing stone, and a young lady, seated. (*Out loud; but hesitant.*) Good evening . . .

Moment's pause.

MRS BEANE. Good evening to you. May I present you to the Countess—

COUNTESS. (*Breaks in in a tumultuous rush.*) Welcome, welcome to my castle. It is so lovely to see a new face, I rarely receive visitors and nothing—nothing, I assure you!—animates me half so much as the presence of a stranger. The castle is so lonely; only the village people come here to bring milk and eggs and a little fresh meat . . . sometimes they bring me a benighted traveller if they should have happened to have stumbled across one. My castle is famed for its hospitality.

Faint rumble of the Count's posthumous chuckle.

You must forgive the shadows . . . my eyes. An affliction of the eyes. I can only see clearly in chiaroscuro, a condition my family shares with the cat. (*During the last few lines the Countess sits in rocking chair.*)

All the following is on thoughts microphone with background continuing.

HERO. At first, in the heavily shaded lamplight, I could hardly make out her features, only her vague shape as it moved a little backwards, a little forwards in a bentwood rocking chair, inexorably as the pendulum of a giant clock; she wears a white muslin dress, she looks like a trapped cloud.

But, as I grew accustomed to the lack of illumination, I distinguished the shocking harmonies of her face.

(*In a brisker, more objective tone.*) The young Countess was so beautiful she might just as well have been hunch-backed; her beauty was so excessive it seemed like a kind of deformity. And I thought, her appearance necessitates her seclusion for even, or perhaps, especially, in her nakedness—

(*Chord of swooning music, continuing during his next sentence.*)—a condition which appalled me even momentarily to contemplate, oh, God, no! not even in her awe-inspiring nakedness!

(*Music ceases abruptly.*) No, even were she to wear only the simplest, most unpretentious, most unbecoming of garments, she would, at any gathering, arrive embarrassingly overdressed. Her beauty was like a dress too good to be worn but, poor girl, it was the only one she had.

COUNT. Her beauty is a symptom of her disorder.

HERO. There was about her not one of those touching little imperfections that reconcile us to the imperfection of the human condition.

COUNT. She is a masterpiece of appearance; she is far too fine an imitation of a woman.

HERO. Her visible inhumanity did not inspire confidence. I had been quite unable to rid myself of the terrible unease that had possessed me since night fell on the Carpathians and, in her lyrical and melancholy presence, I felt it increase to an almost unbearable degree.

Too many shadows in the room might conspire to hide she lacks a shadow.

Her hair falls down inconsolably as rain.

COUNT. She would like very much to be human but, of course, that's quite impossible.

HERO. She is so beautiful she is pitiful.

Her stern, tartan governess has a mouth like a steel trap.

MRS BEANE. (*Brisk, objective, autobiographical.*) My name is Mrs Beane. Widowed early in life, in the most distressing circumstances, left to fend for myself in the wide world with only my five wits and moral fibre to aid me, I answered an advertisement in the Edinburgh Gazette for a governess to a young lady of aristocratic birth in a far corner of the Carpathians. They offered an unusually high salary; but my attention was particularly attracted by the fact that they offered to pay only the one way fare. That is, the fare out.

My interview took place one winter's evening in the drawing room of a luxurious suite at a sumptuous but discreet hotel. Someone I took to be the Count's personal valet, a deaf-mute in a livery of the most funereal black, ushered me into his presence.

Only a little lamp glowed on a corner table yet, in order to shield his over-sensitive eyes from even those few rays it emitted, the Count had donned a green eye-shade. I was to learn that darkness was the exclusive element of this most unfortunate family.

How pale his face was; livid, I should say. Yet, a perfect gentleman. He offered me a chair, he treated me with extraordinary politeness.

After a few preliminary enquiries, he asked me: did I know the Carpathians well? I answered wi' circumspection.

Into drawing-room.

(*In interview with the Count.*) I understand the air is clement. And the mountains generally unfrequented.

COUNT. (*Laughs theatrically.*) Dark, scarcely tenanted forests, a peasantry rooted, rotted deep in the most degrading superstition, vile practices as old as the human race, older . . .

In those rank villages, the Devil himself dances in the graveyards on Walpurgisnacht. A bald mountain, a castle half in ruins . . .

MRS BEANE. (*Thoughts microphone.*) Had I, he asks, rather than an attraction for his phantom-haunted homeland, perhaps, instead, personal reasons for choosing to exile myself so far away from Scotland.

I thought then, och! he must read the newspapers. Maybe he knows more about me than I well ken.

MRS BEANE. (*To the Count.*) Well, sir, I must reluctantly confess . . . that I do have personal reasons . . . of the most pressing nature . . . for wishing to leave Scotland at the first opportunity. And destination, you might say, no object.

COUNT. My daughter, your charge, will not grow up to be . . . as other women. Already, by an exquisite irony, she shows signs of unusual beauty and yet her soul is already darkened by the knowledge of her fate; she is the last bud of a great tree of darkness, the final child of the oldest, most deeply cursed line in all the fatal Balkans . . . blood, blood, blood is her patrimony, Mrs Beane!

Father to son, mother to daughter endlessly the taint leaks back in time . . . the silver bullet, the stake through the heart . . . (*He gasps.*) Ohh!

He pauses to catch his breath and resumes.

Not one of the my house has laid quiet since Vlad the Impaler first feasted on corpses.

MRS BEANE. (*Gasps, recovers herself. Very brisk.*) There's a little taint to every clan, sir. Nobody's perfect. To tell the truth, I guessed there was a snag to the position you have vacant and that's the truth. Such a high salary! And a one-way ticket promised, only the one way. I'd not have answered it had I not been desperate. You see, my husband . . .

COUNT. . . . was recently executed. His crime—

MRS BEANE. I'd never a notion as to the nature of his tastes, married so young as I was. He so cold to me. Then that dreadful night when he came back from the graveyard with his fingernails full of earth and bloated look about him. 'Blood will out,' he said and laughed like a hyena, aptly enough.

COUNT. Necrophagy.

MRS BEANE. Blood will out, the black blood of Sawney Beane, who strewed the beaches outside Edinburgh wi' dead men's bones.

Skirl of bagpipes. Jaunty. Proud.

SAWNEY BEANE. (*Over.*) Times was hard, sheep dying in the field for drought, the landlords grasping, bleeding us white wi' taxes. The corn took blight and rotted in the fields; the plague came, and hunger, worse than plague. We poor folk dying for lack of a crust, ditches crammed with the corpses of the poor. So I says to my Jeannie, the outlaw's life for us! And she says, aye, Sawney, let's eat them up the way they've eaten us.

Bagpipes fade; seagulls, waves.

So Jeannie and I, she being great with child, took ourselves off to the seashore and there we found a cave as high and wide and handsome as the mansion of the Chief Justice and there we lived in comfort. And every passerby on the highroad, first we killed him, then we robbed him and then we ATE HIM UP!

Screaming, wild laughter, cheering, bagpipes again.

And we grew fat and prospered and the bairnies came clustering about my Jeannie's knee, eight fine, strapping sons and six wonderfully blooming daughters. We dressed in silks and satins we pulled off their bodies—skin 'em alive, cried Jeannie! And, oh, she was jewelled like a queen wi' all the gems of the fine ladies whose corpses we subsequently consumed wi' relish, for every night we dined off the fine flesh of earls, barons, marchionesses and so on. The meat had the flavour of excellent pork and you never saw such crackling.

Sounds of meat roasting; children laughing and eating.

In due time, our sons turned to our daughters and knew them and cast new coins from the old moulds while our beaches piled high with dead men's bones. We made our chairs and tables from thigh bones and femurs; we played ducks and drakes with the skulls of the powerful. Our bairnies played five stones wi' vertebrae and learned to count till ten upon phalanges. Och, those were fine days! A great clan of Beanes, seed of my loins, fruit of my Jeannie's womb, roared and ranted through our caves and so we lived and prospered even unto the third generation. And not one child nor one of our children's children ever tasted a scrap of anything but human flesh and flesh of the purest pedigreee. Oh, I was a great anthropophagic patriarch, I was!

Fire burning; seagulls; children's voices; the crunching of bones, fade behind following.

There's nothing to beat the rich flavour of a fat prelate's thigh baked in sea salt over a driftwood fire.

But after five and twenty glorious years, the King's men came for us and there was a mighty battle.

Sword-fighting; women screaming; but Sawney's voice rises up almost in triumph.

We fought like tigers all day long, until the light began to fade and their reinforcements came and so they overwhelmed us, quite, and I and my Jeannie and the tribe that called me father were put to death in Edinburgh, after amazing tortures, amidst scenes of wild rejoicing from the populace.

But we'd eaten more of them than they ever killed of us.

We preyed upon the masters like the wolves upon the flock and so we had our furious triumph!

Screams, shouts, cheers, bagpipes. Fade into child whimpering.

CHILD. Mama? (*No reply.*)
(*Faltering.*) Dada?

SAWNEY BEANE. (*As Mrs Beane's husband.*) The curse of the Beanes. The most insatiable hunger in the world . . .

MRS BEANE. (*Brisk. Thoughts microphone.*) And so I came to take service with the Count, since I was not unfamiliar with the nature of the family's passions. Och! You'd never believe what a pretty wee thing she was, so trusting. How she would cling to me and beg to go out into the garden . . .

Into drawing-room.

COUNTESS AS CHILD. Just this once, Mrs Beane, just this once before sunset . . .

MRS BEANE. (*Younger.*) Wait till the dark, my pet, and then we'll venture out together just a wee way . . .

Owl hoots, followed by a high, thin, prolonged, inhuman scream.

Sobbing.

MRS BEANE. (*Thoughts microphone.*) Her condition seemed to me judgement passed on her long ago, before she was born, my poor, pretty dear. My poor pretty . . .

COUNTESS. (*To hero.*) I am condemned to solitude and dark. I do not mean to hurt you, I do not want to cause you pain. But I am both beauty and the beast, locked up in the fleshly castle of exile and anguish, I cannot help but seek to assuage in you my melancholy . . .

HERO. (*Thoughts microphone.*) A magnificent apartment. Dark tapestries on the walls, a subdued glitter of gold in the ormolu furniture. Here and there a pretty toy, a satin pierrot doll, a figurine of glass, imported from Paris for her, ordered from a catalogue, I daresay. A heavy scent of incense, like a church. Or like a mortician's parlour, for there is something corpse-like about her stillness, as if she were tranced. Her chair moves backwards and forwards but, for herself, she hardly moves at all.

Velvet curtains heavily shut out the night. The Persian carpets demonstrate luminous geometry upon the floor. In her white muslin dress, with the paisley shawl drawn across her frail shoulders and her long, dark hair in gentle disorder . . . she . . .

COUNTESS. (*Whispers.*) Such a fine throat, Mrs Beane, like a column of marble . . .

MRS BEANE. Hush, hush, child. Calm yourself.

COUNTESS. (*Aloud.*) My ancestors suffered very much from the direct rays of the sun and all lived all their lives in these solemn apartments, shaded from the daylight—so many centuries since one of my family saw the sunshine! I've never seen the sunshine though, when I was little, I wanted to. Now, I cannot even imagine what sunshine might be like. When I try to do so, I see only a kind of irradiated dark.

The following on thoughts microphone:

HERO. On her knee a fluffy kitten and on the little table beside her a jewelled cage.

COUNT. I ordered my daughter a jewelled birdcage from Fabergé in Petersburg, for a present on her fifteenth birthday. But when she saw it, she made those signs with her mouth that show how she would like to cry, if only she knew the way.

HERO. In the cage, her pretty bird.

COUNTESS. It is a skylark, its element is morning. But since I've kept it so long in my room, I think it must have grown blind because we keep the curtains drawn all day.

MRS BEANE. You must not give way to self-pity; you are the way you are, a necessary creature of nature, and that's an end to it.

Skylark sings. Over to drawing-room.

COUNTESS AS CHILD. Can a bird sing only the song it knows or can it learn a new song?

MRS BEANE. (*Younger.*) The skylark's song was written out for it when it was hatched, my dear, and, without the intercession of, let us call it "grace" for the sake of argument, may not change its tune by so much as a single sharp or flat.

The following on thoughts microphone:

COUNT. A chignonned priest of the orthodox faith staked me at a certain Slavonic crossroad in the year 1905.

Rapid words in Greek. A blow, a cry.

So end all the line of Vlad the Impaler!

COUNTESS. My destination chose me before I was born. I exist only as a compulsion to repeat it.

Over to drawing-room.

MRS BEANE. Have you come far today, young man?

HERO. (*Hearty.*) From the village in the valley—I fear I can't pronounce it! How unexpected, how splendid! to be amongst English-speakers again! I so much wanted to give the peasants a message about my bicycle but they couldn't make head nor tail of what I was saying, of course.

COUNTESS. Please sit down, there . . . in that deep armchair, beside the fire. Be cosy, please . . . tea . . .

Chink of crockery.

You are just in time for tea.

HERO. (*Thoughts microphone.*) A fine silver service, a kettle on a spirit lamp and cups of such fine china her fingernails tap out carillons as she performs the tea ceremony. She is trying to allay my suspicions. She has put on such an innocent look! My suspicions consist only of an apprehension of the uncanny, and are not soothed by her solicitude.

Drawing-room.

Tea. Yes, milk and sugar, two lumps—thank you.

Chink.

COUNTESS. Will you take a little shortbread? Mrs Beane, my governess, makes it for me herself.

HERO. Shortbread! delicious.

Crunch.

How delicious!

(*Thoughts microphone.*) So here I am in milady's boudoir, with a cup of tea in my hand—good, strong, Indian tea brewed in a silver teapot, not one of those blasted samovars, and in my hand a piece of home-made shortbread—

Drawing-room.

MRS BEANE. We Scotswomen can boast a light hand with pastry. 'The land of cakes,' they call Scotland. Scones and petticoat tails and flapjacks and I don't know what, such teas! When the winter evenings gather in, we bring out the three-tiered cakestand piled high with melt-in-the-mouth home-baking . . .

HERO. (*Thoughts microphone.*) After the Gothic terrors of the early evening, now I find myself taking late tea in a cunning imitation of an Edinburgh drawing-room at five o'clock on a November evening.

How snug. Greenish flames flickering on sweet-smelling apple-logs. How, as the Germans say, gemütlich.

And yet the angel of inquietude stirs her uneasy wings in every corner and I cannot in the least subdue a trembling in my hands. When the tapestry figures shiver in the draught and seem, out of the corner of my eye, to perform the figures of a weird dance, the hairs on my nape helplessly rise . . .

And when she bites her shortbread biscuit—

Crunch.

—I see how curiously pointed her teeth are. Like the teeth of those Melanesians, or Micronesians, or Polynesian islanders who file their canines to a fine point.

Her teeth are too white, too delicate for human teeth. What little light there is in the room shines through her too white, too delicate fingers . . . what long, what pointed nails!
(*More objective tone.*) When I tell you she was the most touching creature I have ever seen, you must realise that this was because her beauty involved the presence of its own absence, implied its own desolating loss, as if it were an uneasy lending.

She implied her own continuous disappearance.
Like a haunting.
A woman is a lonely instrument . . .
How I'm shaking! Unease. Disquiet. Fear? Yes . . . fear.
But not yet . . .
                    . . . quite terrified.

Over to drawing-room.

Kitten purrs; leaps upon hero's knee. Hero starts.

COUNTESS. Oh, puss! What an unexpected honour for you, puss scarcely ever takes to strangers . . .

HERO. (*Recovering his self-possession.*) Pretty, pussy, pretty pussy . . .

Cat begins to purr.

COUNTESS. I have two pets, my cat and my bird; and Mrs Beane takes care of me. But, most of the time, I sleep. I sleep during the daytime, you have just caught me as I wake up. Usually I wake about nightfall, that is the dawn for me. We have an affliction of the eyes in my family, the eyes are inverted, you understand, and so we see best at night. I have an affinity for the cat, for all night creatures, owls . . . beasts that hunt by night.

Distantly, a long, high, lonely, inhuman scream of rabbit or stoat.

HERO. (*Thoughts microphone.*) I thought, perhaps, she was only fifteen or sixteen; but her eyes, the pupils of which were huge as those of all night creatures, contained too much disquiet for so few years. I recognised the high-strung, inbred over-sensitivity, the weakened blood, of an ancient, aristocratic house.

Drawing-room.

Ah, puss! I see you like having your ears tickled.

Cat purrs more loudly.

COUNTESS. Among my terrible forebears, I number the Countess Elizabeth Ba'thory; they called her the Sanguinary Countess. She used to bathe in the blood of young girls to refresh her beauty; she believed these lustrations would keep old age at ay. Look! there is her portrait on the wall, don't you see how little it is. All gilded. An abstract formalisation of her rank rather than a description of her person, don't you think . . . that was the style of the time. She looks rather like . . . an icon.

HERO. (*Thoughts microphone.*) She spoke the word, 'icon', with a cringing temerity, as though the word was usually forbidden her; and her great, sad eyes moved anxiously in her head, as though she were searching for spies in the tapestry, who would be incensed by the word.

I continued to pet the kitten.

Drawing-room. Kitten purring.

COUNTESS. She looks rather like . . . an icon . . . but an icon of unholiness. It shows her looking in a mirror, do you see; but, of course, she couldn't see her own reflection. She is peering and peering in the mirror for her face but she will never find it, never.

The following on thoughts microphone:

Such solitude! to live without one's own reflection.

A genealogy of terror, and of solitude.

MRS BEANE. Her loneliness always tormented her and I could do nothing to console her, only try to convince her, by my continual presence and my resolute inviolability, that she was not indeed inimical to everything human although she'd been born with a full set of teeth, wisdom teeth and all, and every tooth most curiously pointed.

Drawing-room.

Cat purrs more and more loudly; ominous. Suddenly it mews loudly and scratches hero.

HERO. Naughty pussy, naughty—aaaaagh!

Swooping noise, as of wings in an enclosed space.

Aaaaagh!

MRS BEANE. Naughty, naughty—

HERO. (*Thoughts microphone.*) Like a great, white bird, the girl swooped upon me, she, the Countess, you white nightbird, you white butcherbird, spreading your wings, your muslin sails. She swept across the room to fall at my feet, pressing that delicate wet mouth to the juicy wound with ah! such helpless greed. I felt the needles of her cannibal's teeth. I felt the suction of her tongue.

Drawing-room.

Aaaaagh!

MRS BEANE. Countess, oh, but you are a naughty wee thing . . .
(*Thoughts microphone.*) The poor, pretty dear, she can't help it
any more than the kitten could help it. I've grown used to it. At
first, I could hardly bear it . . . those nightwalks in the woods. She
would bound off and come back in a little while with blood on her
dress, making those faces she makes when she wants to cry but
can't, poor wee thing.

HERO. (*Thoughts microphone.*) She drinks as deeply as she can.
Her face is contorted with avidity. Only now, clenched like a leech
to my wrist does she seem truly alive, truly present. She has come
back from wherever it is she goes to and briefly possesses herself.

Then I knew where the fear which inhabits these mountains
makes its home; here, in this perfumed boudoir. Lodged in the
frail flesh of this beautiful young girl.

She drinks as deeply as she may; then, fainting, slips onto the
carpet,

A gentle moan from Countess and rustle as she falls to floor.

lapsed into such torpor the Scotswoman can lift her in her arms as
lightly as if the Countess were made all of rags.

Drawing-room.

MRS BEANE. There, there, my dear. There my, precious.

HERO. (*Thoughts microphone.*) And I, dizzy, sick, can do nothing
but clasp my scratched hand protectively with the whole one and
gaze at the governess with wide eyes of wonder.

Drawing-room.

MRS BEANE. It is her passion. Such has been the dreadful passion
of her house since Vlad the Impaler founded the line. Now she will
sleep a little; she'll return to her almost habitual trance. The valet
will show you to your room.

HERO. (*Faintly.*) My . . . bicycle . . .

MRS BEANE. Och, you'll no be needing that. I fear you'll never leave the castle, young man. We'll send home to your folks that you met an accident somewhere in the Carpathians. We've got it down to a fine art, now, providing for her tastes, covering up the traces. Over and over again we've done it. Over and over.

Now you must rest in your room. I shall not wish you sweet dreams. When she feels the need, she'll come to you.

The following on thoughts microphone:

HERO. The mute in mute's apparel winds me on the little spool of light he carries in his hand through corridors as circuitous as the passages inside the ear. His flame flushes out demented eyes from family portraits along the the galleries; monsters, all . . . Underfoot, worn carpets ripple in the draught . . . a winding staircase of worm-eaten oak . . . I have been here before, in dreams, in nightmares . . .

COUNT. There is no end to the ceaseless cortege of my hospitality.

Key turns in lock.

HERO. Securely locked in, eh? Pleasant room . . . good feather bed. A fine candelabra to light my hours of waiting. And a handsome portrait of Gilles de Raie over the fireplace, if you please! Are the whole damn clan related to every vampire that ever lived!

Well, well, here's a to-do. I shall have to call on all my sang froid to deal with the situation.

A species of trance, of course. Interesting medical condition. I wonder what the sawbones back in London would make of it. Haematodypsia, the pathological thirst for blood . . . an exceedingly rare complaint. Where did I read about haematodypsia . . . And a touch of nervous hysteria, too . . . the young girls' disease. I wonder if the family finances could run to a trip to Vienna, to those Jewboy jennies who stretch you out on a couch and let you tell them how you always wanted to murder your father . . .

Wonder what the governess thinks she's up to. Feudal loyalty, I suppose. Stick to the line of Vlad the Impaler through thick and thin, no matter what . . . even do the Countess's pimping for her, in spite of her Edinburgh rectitude.

Seen queerer things on the North West Frontier, and that's the truth!

All the same, a pretty pickle.

Yet what a lovely creature! Poor, reclusive girl with her weak eyes, and so beautiful . . . . . .

And, round about midnight, pale as water, stooping a little beneath her burden of old guilts, the beautiful somnambulist will turn the key in the door and come into my room on suave, silent feet; she will lay me down upon that narrow bed and feast upon me . . . ah!

Chord of swooning music.

And when I think of that, my shudder is not precisely one of pure terror, although the rational bicycle-rider at war with the pulsing, virginal romantic in my heart tells me I must, in my dealings with this lady, beware, above all else, of masochism.

More things in heaven and earth, Horatio. Do you remember the fakir who rose abruptly into the air, stiff as a board, flat on his back, six feet into the air, suspended without visible support . . . and hung there for fully five minutes, while the crowd wailed?

All to do with breathing . . .

Moment's pause. Into Countess's bedroom.

COUNTESS. Mrs Beane?

MRS BEANE. Just you lie quiet a while.

COUNTESS. Mrs Beane . . . his kisses, his embraces. His head will fall back, his eyes roll. Stark and dead, poor bicyclist; he has paid the price of a night with the Countess and some think it too high a fee while some do not.

MRS BEANE. I will say this, we shall have to get the kitten put down. My, oh, my, pussy, you really gave the game away, didn't you, now! Too soon, too soon . . . she can't resist it, can't resist it for one moment.

The following on thoughts microphone:

COUNT. The sight of blood produces a singular effect on the metabolism of we unfortunates. Not all the jams of paradise spread out upon a table could equal the atrocious appetite the tiniest bead of blood arouses in our febrile senses. Then, only then, do we wake from the curious kind of waking swoon that passes for consciousness amongst us. We seize upon the wound and worry it with our pointed teeth until the liquid life flows down our rabid gullets in torrents, floods . . . drained, empty as a crushed grape, the victim drops to the floor; the wineskin of his body has been emptied and we are fat and drunk upon his life.

ELIZABETH BA'ATHORY. The Sanguinary Countess laved her white, exquisite body in the blood she tapped from the gross veins of peasant girls who had too much blood for their own require-ments. So she kept her wrinkles at bay; she knew how much the preservation of her fabled beauty was worth. Her servants never betrayed her, in spite of torture; they were in such deep complicity with her they urged her to renewed infamies as though her beauty and wickedness were properties of themselves and the more beautiful and wicked she became, the more they, too, were enhanced.

The young girls who became me when they washed me with my awful sponges were as much my victims as those whom I immolated. Yet only in their admiring faces could I see the wonderful results of my magic baths for my piercing eye had broken every mirror in the castle.

When I looked at them, I saw how wonderful I was, and how terrifying.

If they had ceased to be afraid of me, I would have ceased immediately to be beautiful.

I was a great lady and my portrait shows me crusted almost entirely in gold.

SAWNEY BEANE. The landlords were eating us alive and I and my Jeannie, why, we set to upon the landlords! But Jeannie and I, at least we had the common decency to kill our prey first before we devoured it . . . oh, nothing equals a fricassé of Justice of the Peace, served up wi' a fine kelp salad.

HENRI BLOT. Chacun a son gout. Moi, je préfère les cadavres.

Rustle of outrage in court-room; gavel tapped.

COUNTESS. (*Whispering.*) Sometimes Death comes in an erotic disguise; she is your bride . . . she will sheath you in lilies, I am the darkness and solitude from which you come, to which you will go . . .

HENRI BLOT. Each to his fancy . . . Myself, I like corpses.

Rustle of outrage in court-room; gavel tapped.

Yes, your honour, yes your magnanimacy, yes, your serene and objective clemency yes! An honest corpse, with the clean earth still fresh upon her . . . what, you shudder? Your gorge rises?

Hypocrite! When your wife lies beneath your repulsive and importunate body and twists involuntarily away her head so you may not suck upon the open wound of her mouth—immolated alive as she is beneath your judicial weight, my Lord, she who was so young and full of life entombed in your cold house with the children born of no hot passion but only the warmed-over remains of yesterday's unreciprocated lusts, conceived in incidental marital propinquacy alone . . . when you furiously mount the wife whose being you have drained of all fleshly significance, do you not commit a beastly necrophily? A necrophily just as gross as that which I performed upon the dead lilies of the body of Fernande Mery . . .

CLERK OF THE COURT. Professionally known as Carmanio, a ballet dancer.

Rustle of papers.

On the night of March 25, 1886, Henri Blot, aged twenty-six years, scaled a little door leading to the graveyard of St Ouen between the hours of eleven and midnight. He went to one of the trenches where persons not entitled to individual graves were buried and lifted up the boards which held up the earth on the last coffin in the row.

The coffin contained the body of a young woman of eighteen years, Fernande Mery, professionally known as Carmanio, a ballet dancer, buried the preceding evening. He removed the coffin from its resting place, opened it, drew out the corpse and carried it to an open space. He removed the paper wrappings from a number of grave bouquets, spread them upon the ground, and rested his knees upon them so as not to soil his trousers.

BLOT. See—what propriety! What concern for appearances! Can't you tell by just this little gesture towards seemliness what a good bourgeoise I am?

CLERK OF THE COURT. In this position, he obtained carnal intercourse with the corpse. He then slept and did not wake until nearly dawn. On this occasion, he had sufficient time to leave the cemetery unseen but he did not have time to replace the corpse in its grave.

On June 12, Blot again violated a corpse and subsequently slept. On this occasion, he was discovered drowsing beside the defunct and arrested.

BLOT. Corpses don't nag and never want new dresses. They never waste all day at the hairdressers, nor talk for hours to their girlfriends on the telephone. They never complain if you stay out at your club; the dinner won't get cold if it's never been put in the oven. Chaste, thrifty—why, they never spend a penny on themselves! and endlessly accommodating. They never want to come themselves, nor demand of a man any of those beastly sophistications—blowing in the ears, nibbling at the nipples, tickling of the clit—that are so onerous to a man of passion. Doesn't it make your mouth water? Husbands, let me recommend the last word in conjugal bliss—a corpse.

The perfect wife, your honour. Or so, by what I've seen of your good lady, I take it you yourself believe.

CLERK OF THE COURT. The psychiatrists' reports, your honour.

Rustle of papers.

CLERK OF THE COURT. No evidence of insanity . . .

Rustle of papers.

No evidence of insanity . . .

Rustle of papers.

No evidence of insanity . . .

BLOT. Don't they all agree, I'm perfectly normal? We're all in the same boat together!

You, you bourgeois husband striking the pointed stake between your loins into the moist, vital parts of the being who is dependent on your being . . . you, you are the necrophile in your clean white graveclothes! And she, then, what is she, who exists only in the shadow of contingency, a little pale spectre who sucks you dry while you perpetrate infamies upon her . . .

COUNT. The shadow of the fatal Count falls across every marriage bed . . .

Into bedroom.

MRS BEANE. She stirs.

COUNTESS. How handsome he is . . . how the little pulse in his white throat throbs . . .

First, I was content with rabbits or lambs. Then one night, walking in the churchyard, my very sensitive nostrils twitched to sniff the fragrance of a new grave.

The following on thoughts microphone:

MRS BEANE. Rising from her catafalque, the Countess wraps her negligee about her.

So delicate and damned, poor wee thing. Quite damned. Yet I do believe she scarcely knows what she is doing.

Only my bred-in-the-bone, good old Scots hypocrisy keeps me in my position without loss of moral face. I'm secure in my own salvation; I can't alter her destination one little jot.

Hell's her destination; all roads lead her there. So off you go, my pet, and play.

COUNT. One by one, I shall blow out the candles for her . . .

HERO. The little flames flicker and, one by one, go out . . .

COUNT. The clock whirs . . .

Clock whirs.

HERO. Midnight strikes.

Midnight begins to chime. Continues softly while hero speaks.

Only the last little candle left alight, now, bending, dimming yet still not extinguished . . . I do think Milady comes . . .

Chimes cease. Silence. Key softly in door.

COUNT. A waft of cold air, like a blast from a freshly-opened grave, comes into the room with her. She brings this cold wind in her hair, her garments . . .

HERO. The final little flame is reflected in those woundable eyes, shows them rolled upwards, fixed; she does not see the light, I think that now she sees nothing. But her nostrils faintly quiver, so beautiful, so touching in her blood-stained negligee of very rare precious lace.

MRS BEANE. She smells the blood of an Englishman, you ken. Her wee nose goes, twitch, twitch, twitch.

COUNT. Into the world she slipped, through one of the interstices between reality and imagination, the last little twiglet of that genealogical Upas Tree that sprang from the loins of Vlad the Impaler and cast its poison shade over the Balkans for an entire millenium . . . Even the vilest fiends in hell shun the company of the vampire—

COUNTESS. Who is dead yet not dead, whose bane is an insatiable thirst for life and yet an inability to live!

HERO. Grinning, she lunged towards me.

Cry from Countess.

COUNT. Claws and teeth sharpened on several centuries of corpses, sick him, girl, sick him!

Cry, hero grunts.

HERO. I swiftly sidestepped her embrace and caught her by her slender wrist. (*Scuffling.*) How we struggled! Her strength was more than human. But at last I flung her upon my narrow bed and slapped her face, once, on each cheek, the remedy for hysteria. (*Two brisk slaps.*) Although it went against the grain to strike a woman.

COUNT. What? Strike her? Raise your hand to my daughter? To the heiress of the regions of ultimate darkness? To—

But his expostulations are drowned, dwindle away, under the brisk, firm voice of hero.

HERO. The shock did indeed break her trance. Her shoulders quaked; slowly, slowly, she raised her head and turned those eyes the shape of tears laid on their sides towards me. Her features twisted. Although her eyes were shaped like tears, she could not weep. Nevertheless, she continued to try to do so. Perhaps her whole life had been a balked attempt at crying.

Bedroom acoustic.

COUNTESS. I am not a demon, for a demon is incorporeal; nor a phantom, for phantoms are intangible. I have a shape; it is my own shape, but I am not alive, and so I cannot die. I need your life to sustain this physical show, my self. Please give it to me.

HERO. (*Thoughts microphone.*) Her rich lips part; she smiles, she raises herself, she beckons.

I felt myself seized by the most powerful erotic attraction; only the exercise of iron self-control prevented me from throwing myself at her little feet.

Yet I, who love the bicycle and the light of common day, cannot, in the final analysis, bring myself to partake in this grisly charade. My reason forbids it.

Bedroom.

COUNTESS. My life depends on yours. I am a woman, young and beautiful. Come to me.

HERO. (*Thoughts microphone.*) And so she folds herself upon the bed with the lace falling about her softly and stretches out her white arms to me, her long hands with those fingernails like mandolin-picks . . . I blessed the cold showers of my celibacy. (*Into bedroom. Addresses Countess.*) Countess, keep your talons to yourself.

COUNT. What? What?

HERO. (*Thoughts microphone.*) When I held her wrists together to keep her murderous hands away from me, she made her weeping face and writhed a little, for she was thwarted, poor, spoiled child. (*Into bedroom. Addresses Countess.*) When I first saw you tonight, I thought you were an infinitely pitiable creature because of your beauty and your loneliness.

COUNT. (*Thoughts microphone.*) Curious . . . now she seems to wake. Her eyes clear; they settle upon him. How pure and pale his lips are, lips that have never—oh, never! Oh, can it be—

Bedroom.

COUNTESS. (*To hero.*) My father loved me and brought Mrs Beane over the sea from Scotland to look after me. He taught me how to suck the blood from the young rabbits and crunch so deliciously their little bones as we crouched in the moist undergrowth of the thickets by the churchyard.

But I grew up and then I was not satisfied with the rabbits and the baby lambs and the little calves still wobbling on their newborn legs. No. Now I must have men. And so they come, but never go. All dead.

All dead.

I know I only lodge within my body; I am I and yet not I, as if I haunted my own shape and am condemned to watch with shame and rage its beastly doings.

HERO. Look! She is trying to cry, again.

COUNTESS. My kith's relations with my kind exiles me from daylight.

I am a creature of the night, only.

(*In a subtly different tone of voice.*) I belong to the night.

HERO. (*Thoughts microphone.*) One thin, wandering hand muzzles the ribbons of her negligee. She slips succinctly from the garment and relapses upon the coverlet in the most alluring abandon. In my head, I hear all the string orchestras of seduction playing at once together.

So she voluptuously invites me to step into Juliet's tomb.

And I was foolish enough in my rationality to set out upon a bicycle tour of the Carpathians with none of the traditional impedimenta of the vampire hunter about me, no wreath of garlic, no silver bullet . . . But only the conviction this is a poor, sick girl maintains me in the perpendicular stance of reason when common sense tells me the best thing to do in the circumstances is to fling myself helplessly upon her . . .

Chord of swooning music; which breaks off abruptly in the middle.

Bedroom.

(*To Countess, briskly but tenderly.*) We should take you away to Vienna, where doctors could examine you. You would stretch out on the therapeutic couch and the stern, quiet, bearded physician would tease from you during the slow intervals of healing time the confused origins of your sickness.

COUNTESS. Why aren't you afraid of me? Why don't you shrink from my murderous fingers.

HERO. What can your governess be thinking of, never to have cut your nails. You fine lady with your Strewelpeter's hands.

COUNTESS. They cripple the feet of Chinese women, as a sign of status. It is the same with me; I may not use my hands as hands. Three inches of horn stick out at the tips, don't you see . . . useless for anything but gouging.

The following on thoughts microphone:

HERO. With an infinitely touching gesture, she tucked her hands away behind her back, as though she were ashamed of them, and smiled at me, tremulously.

COUNT. (*Faintly.*) My daughter, oh, my daughter! am I losing you?

HERO. With no thought of passion, heaven forbid! Only of consolation, I took her in my arms.

Bedroom.

Countess cries out in surprise; the cry protracts into a sigh.

COUNTESS. How warm you are, how you warm me . . .

COUNT. (*Thoughts microphone.*) I find it . . . difficult . . . to breathe. My little girl! Don't you remember me? don't your remember sucking the delicious bones of the baby rabbits?

Bedroom.

COUNTESS. I never, in all my life, felt warm till now.

HERO. (*Thoughts microphone.*) She leans her head upon my shoulder with the most moving simplicity and I gently stroke her disordered hair.

Bedroom.

COUNTESS. If I sang you my leibestod, you would not understand it.

HERO. I never liked Wagner. Heavy, decadent stuff. Do you think you could sleep, my dear?

COUNT. . . . Choking . . . Airless . . .

HERO. (*Thoughts microphone.*) She's rich enough to pay for treatment, in all conscience. Oh, the poor girl. A ghastly affliction.

Bedroom.

COUNTESS. I feel . . . almost a healthy sleepiness come upon me. Will you . . . would you . . . could you give a goodnight kiss?

The following on thoughts microphone:

Count moans.

HERO. I was infinitely moved.
   Softly, with my lips, I touched her forehead, as if I had been kissing a child goodnight.

COUNT. His pure, pale lips on your brow—ah! Fall upon me all at once the consecrated sword, the pointed stake!

Juicy thud. Count screams.

COUNTESS. I always knew that love, true love would kill me.

COUNT. . . . aaargh . . .

HERO. She felt quite limp in my arms, as if after the crisis of a fever. Soon it will be morning; the crowing of the mundane cock and first light will dissolve this Gothic dream with the solvent of the natural. Yes, perhaps I shall take her to Vienna; and we shall clip off her fingernails and take her to a good dentist, to deal with her fangs.
   Perhaps, perhaps . . . one day, when she is cured . . . mother, I want you to meet . . .

He is growing sleepy, too. The Count moans and gurgles.

COUNT. Is a millenium of beastliness to expire upon a *kiss*?

HERO. There are some things that, even if they are true, we must not believe them.

Moaning fades.

COUNTESS. I existed only . . . as a symbolic formula. I was a woman, young and beautiful.

HERO. A little curl dangles over her forehead and moves with her breathing . . . sweet. So sweet. Oh, I don't believe your silly tales . . . just the hysteria of a young girl. In this isolated place, at the back of beyond, with only the family portraits for company.

Look, now she sleeps deeply.
(*Yawns.*) Could do with a spot of shut-eye myself. Been a heavy day.

Yawns again. Silence. Sleeping breathing. Last, faint moan from the Count.

Cock-crow.

When I awoke, refreshed, I found I was clasping in my arms only a white lace negligee a little soiled with blood, as it might be from a woman's menses.

Over to drawing-room.

Cage is opened.

MRS BEANE. Fly away, birdie, fly away!

Lark song.

HERO. (*Approaching.*) Why, Mrs Beane, you've opened up the curtains! My goodness, what a view!

Windows are opened.

MRS BEANE. Let a breath of fresh air into this mausoleum . . . A glorious morning. I sent a man to look after your bicycle. You'll be wanting to get on with your tour, after you've had your breakfast.

HERO. The Countess . . .

MRS BEANE. I regret most bitterly you should have visited us at a time of mourning. The last of the line, you understand . . . they'll say Mass for her in the chapel. I myself, being a freethinker, will not attend. I am well provided for in the will, of course. I shall return to Scotland as soon as the estate has been wound up and open a girls' finishing school, perhaps. Or a boarding house. (*Pawky humour.*) *Not* a mutton pie shop, you'll be glad to hear.

HERO. May I see—

(*Thoughts microphone.*) In the last repose of death, she looked a little older but not much, a good deal uglier since she had lost all her teeth and, because of her loss of allure, for the first time, fully human.

Bicycle wheels on a stony track. Birdsong.

So I sped through the purged and rational splendours of the morning; but when I arrived at Bucharest, I learned of the assassination at Sarajevo and returned to England immediately, to rejoin my regiment.

Drum-beats; above, the Count's dreadful, posthumous chuckle.

COUNT. The shadow of the Fatal Count rises over every bloody battlefield.

Everywhere, I am struck down; everywhere, I celebrate my perennial resurrection.

PUSS
IN BOOTS

Fade in Figaro's aria from 'The Barber of Seville', take down behind:

ANNOUNCER.—

Bring up music and fade.
Dead acoustic.

PUSS. Ladies and gentlemen, a very good good day to you, and I hope you enjoy the show as much as we enjoy—what? what's the big joke? (*He's engaging with an inaudible heckler.*) Never seen a cat before, is that it? Never been addressed *as an equal* by a cat before? . . . and is it any wonder . . .

Well, I daresay that . . . you've never met a cat like me! Feline and *proud*, ladies and gentlemen. Felis domesticus by genus—that is, for those of you who don't speak Latin, a short-haired domestic ginger. In short, a marmalade cat. Male. *Whole* male. Oh, yes, indeed! This handsome, furred and whiskered person standing here before you tonight has much to be proud of. Proud, for a start, of his white shirtfront, or dickey, dazzling the eye, forming an elegant, formal contrast to the orange, tangerine and amber tessellations of the rest of my coat, my pelt, my brilliant uniform which is as fiery to the eye as is the the the suit of lights worn by the matador . . . Such a tom as I may well be proud, too, of his bird-entrancing eye and more than military whiskers; proud—

HERO. —to a fault—

PUSS. —of my superbly musical voice. When I break into impromptu song at the spectacle of the moon above Bergamo, my native city, scene of the events about to befall—when I spontan-eously serenade the moon above Bergamo, all the windows in the square fly open—

Fade in exterior, empty square. Cat howling; windows open-ing; angry murmurs swelling to furious exclamations.

CITIZEN'S WIFE: (*Off.*) 'eave 'arf a brick at 'im!

CITIZEN. (*Off.*) 'eave it yourself.

2ND CITIZEN. (*Off.*) Shoot 'im!

3RD CITIZEN. (*Off.*) Bomb 'im!

4TH CITIZEN. (*Off.*) Nuke 'im!

Take cat howling and angry cries down behind following:

PUSS. When the poor players set up their stage here in the square, they think themselves lucky if the parsimonious Bergamots toss them a few, paltry pence. But I—when *I* start to sing, how liberally my grateful public rewards me with deluges of pails of the freshest water—

Splash.

—often they dower me with new-laid—well, fairly new-laid— eggs, and the succinctly ripest of the tomato crop—

Splatter.

—sometimes even slippers, shoes—

HERO. (*Off.*) Take that, you caterwauling fiend!

Crash.

(*Off.*) And that!

Crash.

PUSS. Boots! A pair of boots! What generosity! What a tribute! What a splendid gift! Fine, high, leather boots polished so brilliantly I can see my face in them . . . hi, there, Puss, you're looking *good*, tonight, good . . . Such boots! I wonder . . . will they fit me?

Rapturous purring. Take down behind following:

HERO. (*Narrating.*) When blessed peace fell on the square outside my lodging and all the disturbed Bergamots had gone back to bed, I looked out of the window to see what had become of my boots . . . and there, below me, to my infinite astonishment, the very strangest sight I ever beheld . . .

Bring up square and purring as heard from window of hero's room.

PUSS. (*Off.*) Perfect fit. Purrfect . . .

Take down background.

HERO. .... there was a cat, presumably the perpetrator of the ghastly serenade that had moved me to felinocidal violence, a great big ginger tom of formidable size and length of tail, engaged, of all things, in pulling on, over his hind paws, those very boots that I had just before, in my fury, hurled at him.
(*Calling.*) Hey! Puss? What are you up to?

PUSS. (*Off.*) Fit like a glove, sir! Merci!

HERO. Merci? Why does he thank me in French?

PUSS. (*Off.*) It's the only language in which you can purr, sir.

HERO. You strike me as a cat of parts. Let's see how well you can climb in those boots.

PUSS. (*Off.*) Climb?

HERO. Up to my balcony!

PUSS. (*Off.*) Nice rococo facade to the place . . . rococo's a piece of cake for a cat, sir, either booted or barefoot.

HERO. (*Narrating.*) With that, the remarkable creature proceeded to scale the exterior of my lodgings. First, he rose up on his hind legs to his full height, which I judged to be some three or four feet—

PUSS. (*Narrating.*)—three feet eleven inches, call it four foot, not including my tail, that is. You never get it right; let's be precise just this once, for the record, okay? Can we attempt, perhaps, to be scrupulous, tough as it is on you?

HERO. (*Narrating.*) Listen to the way he speaks to me! As though I were a child and he were my nanny! Truly, since I first met him, I could hardly call my life my own; I—

PUSS. (*Off.*) Here! I say! Going to leave me half way up to the balcony, are you? Going to leave me here all night, are you, while you complain and whinge and moan when all you have you owe to me? Going to abandon me hanging here, are you?
    What will happen to your blooming story, then?

HERO. (*Sigh.*) Very well. (*Making amends.*) With a sinuous ripple of marmalade muscle—

PUSS. (*Narrating, approving.*)—nice touch—

HERO. (*Narrating.*)—he set his forepaws on the carved pate of a curly cherub that decorated the lower part of the facade and, not one whit discommoded by the boots which he had donned, he brought his back paws up to meet them. Then—

PUSS. (*Climbing.*)—first paw forward, hup! to the stone nymph's tit, left paw down a bit, this . . . satyr's bum should . . . do the trick . . . nothing to it once you know how. I was born to acrobatics, born to them. And very, very often have I performed, in return for a bit of salt cod or the pope's nose off a goose, to the applause of all, a perfect back somersault whilst holding a glass of vino in my right paw and never spill a single drop!

HERO. Not one drop?

PUSS. (*Narrating.*) I see the young man is impressed by my talents. I forebear to inform him, therefore, that, to my shame, I never yet attempted the famous death-defying *triple* somersault that is the greatest trial and test of such ambitious acrobats of the style of I.

The young man welcomes me in through the window with a friendly chuck under the chin.

Soft thump of cat jumping into room; purr.

HERO. Amazing performance . . .

PUSS. (*Narrating.*) . . . and offers me, polite as anything . . .

HERO. A sandwich?

PUSS. (*Narrating.*) Roast beef, just how I like it, lean, moist, pink, easy on the mustard . . .

Eating noises.

HERO. (*Narrating.*) But all the time I plied the cat with sandwiches, I pondered how to get my boots back.
(*In room.*) A snifter of brandy, perhaps?

PUSS. (*Mouth full.*) Won't say no, sir. I've a great liking for a spot of ardent spirits, picked up the taste in the vintners—I started out in life as a cellar cat, right here, in the city of Bergamo. One fine day, curled up in an empty barrel, overcome with fumes, nodded off, next thing I knew, woke up in Genoa—took service as a ship's cat, learned to roll my r's in Marseilles, to caterwaul in Spain . . .

Glass filled.

It's been a full life. Fill the glass right up to the top, sir—

More pouring.

Keep out the cold. Chilly, tonight, sir. Winter draws on. (*He downs drink in one, smacks lips.*) Got a drop more of that?

HERO. (*Narrating.*) When I saw the way the cat knocked back the brandy, I realised my plan to render him insensible and then remove my boots was inappropriate. I noticed he was examining my appearance extremely closely . . .

PUSS. By your coat, I see you're a military man, sir. Cavalry, eh?

HERO. (*Embarrassed.*) I—ah. Yes. I—

PUSS. Past tense, is it? *Was* a military man? When was you cashiered, sir?

HERO. Another—beef sandwich. Oh.

PUSS. I ate it already, in anticipation of your invite. Cards, was it? Or women? Or a combination of both, plus, perhaps, duelling and the juice, sir? And how does it earn its living, now?

HERO. (*Narrating.*) I saw I could keep no secrets from this cat . . . (*In room.*) To be perfectly frank with you, Puss, I go in for a little card-sharping, a little gaming, a little bit of this and that, you understand; and I live simply, in these lodgings, here . . . and I have but the one pair of boots . . .

PUSS. Which you so kindly, so very kindly! gave to me. And I shall cherish them always. And, in order to repay you, I shall move in with you—

HERO. —what?

PUSS. Don't you ever feel the need of a valet?

HERO. A valet?

PUSS. A valet.

HERO. (*Thoughtfully.*) A valet!

PUSS. A touch more brandy, to seal the bargain?

HERO. A valet . . .

Hero pours drink.

Do you know, I can see . . . all manner of ways . . . in which you'd make the perfect valet, Puss. Purrfect . . . your health!

Clinks glasses.

PUSS. (*Narrating.*) And I daresay the Master and I have much in common, for he's proud as the devil—

HERO. Say that again and smile!

PUSS. (*Narrating.*)—touchy as tin-tacks—

HERO. Swords or pistols?

PUSS. (*Narrating.*)—as lecherous as liquorice—

GIRL. Oh! oh . . . oh! . . . oh!! . . . oh!!!

PUSS. (*Narrating.*)—in short, as quick-witted a rascal as ever changed his shirt.
So Puss got his post at the same time as his boots and then it was busy, busy, busy . . .

Fade in Figaro's aria.

It was Figaro, here, Figaro, there, I tell you! Figaro upstairs, Figaro, downstairs, and oh, my goodness me! this little Figaro can slip into my lady's chamber smart as you like at any time of the day or night for what lady in all the world of any age, complexion or disposition could say no to my advances, to the passionate, indefatigable yet *toujours discrets* attentions of a marmalade cat . . .

Sneeze, which cuts short music. Hag's room.

HAG. Sod off, bugger off, get the hell out of it, you miserable cat—

PUSS. Get the hell out of it yourself, you old hag—you don't come in till later, anticipated your cue again—

Fade on sneeze.

HERO. (*Narrating.*) Although I felt that the servant had chosen the master rather than the more conventional way about, I soon found myself wondering how I could ever have managed without him. He was a valet beyond price—

Hero's room.

PUSS. Is that why you don't pay me, sir?

HERO. Don't I share all that I have with you?

PUSS. Which means, all that I steal.

HERO. So you've brought home some breakfast! Where is it, let's see . . . an orange, a loaf . . . and what's that you're hiding behind your back? Come on, let's have it—

Scuffle.

A herring!

PUSS. (*Narrating.*) The master chopped up this herring very fairly in order to make two servings, for first he cut the head off—

Chop.

and then the tail—

Chop.

and popped the meaty bit in between into the frying pan—

Sizzle.

for he never could get it into his thick skull that a cat's not choosy as to whether its breakfast is cooked or raw. So, while he was slicing his bread—

Mew; fish removed from pan; eating sounds.

HERO. Puss!

PUSS. (*Mouth full.*) Share and share alike, sir! Ain't I left you the head and the tail?

HERO. (*Narrating.*) I could scarcely escape the notion, sometimes, that as soon as my new valet had insinuated his way into my life, I myself had lost complete control of it . . .

Fade in casino.

But as soon as we stepped into the casino together, I would forgive him anything; for a cat may move with impunity from one lap to another—

Purring.

GAMBLER. Why, whom do we have here? Of all things, a cat— puss, puss, pretty puss . . .

Purring.

HERO. (*Narrating.*) I never go anywhere without my mascot, my lucky charm, my portable good fortune . . .

GAMBLER. Why, puss, my goodness me, you do like to be stroked and petted . . . don't you? Yes . . .

Re-doubled purring.

PUSS. (*Sotto voce.*) . . . an ace, a king, a ten and a queen, gottit?

HERO. (*Narrating.*) If he was an invaluable extra pair of eyes at a card game, he performed a rather more dramatic function when it was a game of dice—

Rattle; cat hunting cry; puss jumps with a thud on the dice; exclamations of gamblers.

Oh! the poor creature can't resist it when he sees the dice roll! Mistook them for mousies, didn't you, you silly old thing . . .

PUSS. (*Narrating.*) And after he scoops me up all limp-spined and stiff-legged as I am, playing the cat-idiot, and he chastises me, then, oh! who can remember how the dice fell in the first place?

HERO. Heaven smiles on me tonight! A double six!

PUSS. (*Narrating.*) And we had, besides, less . . . gentlemanly . . . means of support to which he was forced whenever—

Cut casino.

HERO. (*Narrating.*) Banned from the tables again, dammit! And my cat, too, my little lucky cat? What do you mean, especially the cat . . .

PUSS. (*Narrating.*) At such times as these, when the cupboard was bare as his backside, when, in short, the poor soul had been forced to pawn his drawers . . .

Flamenco guitar.

—you must know that all cats have a Spanish tinge—

Flamenco singer. Cross to exterior square.

—down to the square we'd go and there I'd do the Spanish dance I'd learned in Catalonia—

Flamenco; bootheels.

—stamping the ground in my boots, olé!

HERO. (*In square.*) Buenos gracias, senora; buenos gracias, senor . . .

Chink of money exchanging hands; bootheels; flamenco; conclude with flourish on loud chord and applause. Fade.

PUSS. (*Narrating.*) So Puss and his Man rubbed along famously together and all went right as ninepence until—

Fade in silent movie 'Hearts and Flowers' music.

—until, alas—

HERO. (*Narrating.*) . . . with one smile she conjured the heart out of my bosom . . . when I first saw her smile, it was as if this heart of mine, this frequently abused, rarely if ever seriously touched organ in my bosom, my heart . . . my heart sprouted wings that instant and fluttered across the square to hover around her, like a butterfly just out of the chrysalis, tenderly, tremulously . . .

PUSS. —until the man goes and falls in love.

Fade 'Hearts and Flowers' music.

In love!

SEVERAL WOMEN'S VOICES ALL TOGETHER. (*Agitated, astonished, mocking.*) In love? In love! In love . . .

HERO. (*Firm.*) In love.

PUSS. (*Narrating.*) And needs must he chooses to fall in love with the single individual most inaccessible woman in all Bergamo. In love with her at first sight of her smiling face.

And that face, in itself, the most uniquely unlikely sight in the whole city.

HEROINE. (*Narrating.*) I am the wife of Signor Pantaleone. I am young and beautiful and it is my misfortune to have been married against my will out of the schoolroom as payment for bad debts to a bald, gouty miser whose red nose bristles with hairy warts, a grotesque and sinister ancient old enough to be my father—my *grandfather*! A man as jealous as he is incompetent, who keeps me locked up like a holy statue and scarcely lets me see the light of day.

PANTALEONE. (*Narrating.*) Now, now, be fair! Don't I let you have a full hour every evening at your bedroom window? One full hour! What if·you *do* have to keep a sack over your head, the while, so, though you can look out, nobody can look in at you—I don't display my prized possessions to the public, I don't waste them on any old Tom, Dick or Harry, oh, no!

Bring in distant square during following, as heard from heroine's room.

HEROINE. (*Narrating.*) For one hour, for one hour only, at the tenderest time of dusk, in the obscure light of early evening, then he allows me, half-hidden by the curtains, to open the shutters and look down on the busy doings of the square, the dancers on ropes, the women selling cabbage and water melons, the hurly burly of life from which I am in exile. I can look out provided I am securely tied.

PANTALEONE. (*In room.*) Oh yes, I have her on a string. Keep a string round her ankle, tether her . . .

HERO. (*Narrating.*) Sometimes I saw the open window, like the dark mouth of a cave, but I never saw you—

HEROINE. No—

HERO. —not until—

Bring in church bells.

PANTALEONE. I even let her go to Mass on Sundays!

HEROINE. (*Narrating.*) Yes; on Sunday mornings, very early, when only the most godly venture out, he allows me out of the house for a brief interview with my maker, although you would think my husband more a Turk than a Christian by the way he makes me parcel up in veils. And, of course, I'm never permitted to venture out alone . . .

PANTALEONE. (*Narrating.*)—Who knows what she might get up to, then? Young women, young women . . . cunning as monkeys. To police my wife's piety, I employ, as her constant companion, a trusted lady of mature years who has been long in my employ.

HAG. (*Narrating.*) I am her governess.

HEROINE. (*Narrating.*) She is my wardress.

PUSS. (*Narrating.*) And so it came to pass as how the lovely wife of Signor Pantaleone was on her way to Mass and my master glimpsed her face by accident, one morning, one Sunday morning, so early of a Sunday morning that, for those of us who go to bed as late as my man and I, it was still night time . . .

Bring up bells as heard from exterior street. Footsteps on cobbles.

HERO. (*Narrating.*) We'd played at cards so late, made such a killing at the tables that the pious ones were already making their way to church through the cold, dark fog as we went home—

PUSS. —our pockets a-chink with ill-gotten gains and our guts a-sweetly-gurgle with champagne . . . (*Hiccups.*) Out of the front door of Pantaloon's mansion comes two women . . .

Two sets of footsteps approach; rustle of dresses; one woman breathing heavily.

PUSS. . . . an old woman . . .

HAG. (*In street.*) . . . filthy cold, this morning; filthy fog; black as a bucket, this morning, too—filthy, filthy . . .

HERO. (*Narrating.*) . . . the other a tall, slender figure, like a stem of narcissus, but all wrapped up in black . . .

PUSS. (*Narrating.*) . . . she making a graceful and stately progress, though all muffled up in crepe like a mourning doorknocker. And I, having had, I must admit, a couple . . .

HEROINE. (*In street.*) Oh, Puss! Good morning!

PUSS. (*Narrating.*) . . . thinks I'll exercise myself with a game of tag with the dangling fringe of her shawl . . .

HEROINE. Does Pussy want to play?

HAG. Filthy cat! I can't abide—atishoo—get away, you filthy cat! Atishoo! (*She sneezes and continues to sneeze.*)

HEROINE. Take no notice of my governess, Puss. Her nostrils tickle at the flick of a whisker. But as for myself, I'm very fond of cats . . . do you know my Tabs? My stripey Tabs? H'm? Oh my, what a handsome cat you are . . . and so very, very friendly . . .

Purr.

Does he like his ears tickled? Just here—is that the ecstatic spot?

Purr.

PUSS. (*Narrating.*) . . . And then I couldn't help myself . . .

HEROINE. What a somersault! A double somersault! Well! But—whatever have you got on your hind feet . . .

PUSS. (*Narrating.*) And so she drew her veil aside to see.

HEROINE. Puss in boots!

Laughter.

HERO. (*Narrating.*) When she drew back her veil, suddenly, it was May morning—

Electronic birdsong; few notes on a harp.

HAG. ATISHOO!

That puts a stop to the harp and birdsong.

Drat the nasty beast! Put it down, you don't know where it's been . . . and down with your veil this instant, don't want any of the rag-tag and bobtail to see you! Quit dawdling—come along!

HEROINE. Don't pull so—oh! you're bruising my arm!

Rustle of departing dresses; a chill wind rises and blows them away.

PUSS. (*Shivering.*) Brrr . . . nasty nip in the air all of a sudden.

HERO. How cold it is. And dark. Now that she's gone. She has taken all the promise of spring with her.

Fade background. Brief pause.

PUSS. And so my master fell in love.

HERO. Head over heels!

PUSS. Positively the double, nay, possibly even the triple somersault of the heart, eh?

HERO. Without a safety net.

PUSS. Without a partner! She doesn't even know your name.

HERO. She is a princess imprisoned in a tower, remote and shining as Aldebaran, chained to a dolt, guarded by dragons . . .

PUSS. By one dragon. Or, rather, a dragoness.

Room acoustic. Distant square.

HERO. (*Moving slightly off to window across bare boards.*) When I sit here, at the window of my room, I can see her house across the square, the locks, the bolts, the barred windows . . . I sit, and sit, and gaze, and gaze . . . oh, the sweet tyranny of love . . . until that moment, once a day, when I can make out her vague shape, like the moon behind clouds—

PUSS. (*Aside.*) Hark at him, babbling on about the tender passions! Has he come to this, he the witty and ingenious lecher who went through all the novices in the *entire convent*, Puss passing in and out the cloister with notes, roses, boxes of chocolate etc. etc. etc. until my very whiskers smelled of incense. Is he reduced to impotent yearning, the notorious rake who had the Mayor's wife under the table at the conclusion of the Mayor's banquet while they served the madeira? This—

HERO. (*Slightly off.*) Cynic.

PUSS. You only want her because you can't have her, you spoiled brat. The poor girl might just as well live in a bank vault as in the finest mansion in Bergamo, and you don't know the combination to her safe.

And, speaking of money, sir, you should know that we're running a mite short on funds . . . temporary cash-flow problem, sir, which would easily and speedily be resolved by a visit to the gaming tables—

HERO. (*Slightly off.*) No, Puss; not today . . . it's nearly half past four. She'll open her windows presently . . . and perhaps today the Hag will accidentally agitate the curtain as she picks at a pimple, she may even dislodge the curtain sufficiently to let me see the lady's hands, her hands, all that can be seen of her, white hands, like lilac on a coffin . . .

PUSS. (*Aside.*) . . . enough to make you queasy . . .

HERO. And then, an early night; tomorrow, up bright and early—to Mass! Thank God for Sunday!

PUSS. For, would you believe it, the reprobate has now taken to attending church regular as prunes.

HERO. Perhaps, tomorrow, if we sit in the pew behind her, I shall manage, when we kneel, to touch the hem of her dress . . .

Organ music cuts distant square background. Church acoustic. Rustling; sneeze.

HAG. (*Angry whisper.*) I could swear there was a cat about; I—atishoo!

HEROINE. Hush, governess, control yourself . . . whoever would bring a cat to church?

HAG. Atishoo!

Crossfade organ music to congregation leaving church.

HERO. Look!

PUSS. A glove.

HERO. Hers. She left it lying on the pew.

PUSS. How do you know it's her glove and not the hag's glove?

HERO. Because it's so little, such tiny hands but—see! Long fingers; and it smells sweet . . . her perfume . . . exquisite, scented hands, hands to caress a man, to console . . .

Fade background behind following:

PUSS. (*Narrating.*) And all day long he babbled these and similar maudlin sentiments sufficient, as they say, to make a cat laugh, and soon our common purse is flat as a pancake for this new-found unrequited passion of his has suddenly afflicted him with scruples.

Hero's room.

HERO. I'll never load the dice nor palm a card again. I'll keep my hands from picking and stealing. She, she'd never look at a cheat, or a thief . . .

PUSS. (*Narrating.*) So my master is in a fair way to ruin us both by neglecting his business due to the unsatisfied ravages that LOVE is making upon his constitution.

Now, since my observation of the human species has led me to opine that love is nothing but desire sustained by unfulfilment, I therefore conclude that . . . if I can by guile and cunning . . . effect a physical consummation of this young man's debilitating passion, he'll forthwith be right as rain in two shakes and next day tricks as usual. And Puss and his Man soon solvent once again.

Which, at the moment, very much not, sir.

Pause.

Now, this Tabs to whom the young lady had referred, turns out to be the house mouser her miserable husband employs, a sleek, spry, short-haired domestic tabby of the feminine gender . . .

Fade in Rossini's cat duet—the duet of the two cats singing together; fade slowly, leaving behind heavy, contented breathing. Close acoustic.

TABS. Well! You are a one and no mistake!

What a hearty greeting from a new-found friend! I tell you straight, the young missus could do with a bit of what you've just given me. Oh, yes, that'd put the roses back in her cheeks, all right.

Poor, lonely lady, as she is, tied for life to that gore-bellied old dodderer, lean and slippered, eyes like a boiled cod only not half so appetising, with his pot leg and his nose going drip-drip-drip like a faulty tap and the hands of his clock always at half past six d'you get my meaning I see you get my meaning and parsimonious! You wouldn't believe. My dear, does he budget for so much as a scrap of anchovy for yours truly? Does he 'ell! Keeps me on short commons for the sake of the mousing, grasping old skinflint as he is.

PUSS. Ma pauvre chérie . . .

TABS. If it wasn't for the young lady, bless her heart, slipping into the kitchen to smuggle me the odd chicken wing, knuckle of mutton, backbone of haddock, I'd be the skinniest tabs in all Bergamo—

PUSS. —instead of the glossiest, plumpest, brightest-eyed little—

TABS. (*Pleased, all the same.*) Go on! I've met your sort. Where was I . . . She's a lovely lady, the missus, lovely; but ooh! that governess of hers!

PUSS. The governess, the hag, the dragoness.

TABS. Apart from her generally unattractive personality and repulsive appearance, she and I never hit it off, not really. See, soon as ever she sniffs so much as a whiff of me, she's off—atishoo! atishoo! Veritable paroxysms.

'Course, I used to love to lie in wait for her behind the parlour door, or curled up on her pillow, if I got the chance, just to tease the old girl, but then she started up such a clamour about her allergies, and the torments I caused her, got to get rid of the cat, she said . . . talked about popping me in a sack and taking me to the river, murderous old cow.

PUSS. She never did!

TABS. She did so. But the young lady put her foot down, told the hag if she didn't give over she'd tell the old one how the hag scrapes the whitewash off the privy wall and uses it to powder her horrible old face with—they're two of a kind, the pantaloon and the hag, mean as hell, he'd have had out on her arse for chronic thievery for that! Before you could say Jack Robinson.

So then the hag piped down.

Oh, that young lady! She saved my life. But apart from that, many's the time we sneak a game of hunt-the-cotton-reel and jump-on-the-handkerchief together, when we get the chance . . . when she is with me, the hag leaves her alone.

Yes, I would say we are the only ray of sunshine in one another's lives.

Until you popped up out of the coal hole like a good deed in a naughty world, Mr Marmalade!

Purring.

PUSS. What say . . . we hatch a plot . . . to antler the old one, darling Tabs?

TABS. You're on! Now you're talking! Do you know, would you believe, that I never, ever heard her bedsprings rattle, not since the poor thing's wedding day . . . not so much as a single twang . . . To him, she is no more than his most prized possession, and a bargain, too, got her cheap off her father due to a mortgage falling in.

But antlering is easier said than done, my old cock, me ginger-winger, me Tim-Tam-Tom. All day and every day, he sits in his counting-house counting out his money and doesn't budge an inch from his securities . . . and he keeps his what you might call *tabs* on her even when she's with me, would you believe he keeps a string tied all the time from his great toe to the lady's ankle so she can't move an inch without him knowing?

Fade in counting house.

PANTALEONE. . . . just check up on the girl . . .

HEROINE. (*Off.*) Oh!

Back to close acoustic.

PUSS. He sits in his counting house all day and every day?

TABS. I tell a lie! Silly old me—Wednesdays! Of course—he clears out just the one day a week. Wednesdays. Then he forsakes his wife and coffers to ride out into the country and extort grasping rents from starveling tenants, since he won't trust a bailiff to do the job for him.
    But that one day a week he shoots so many bolts on her—

Shooting bolts.

and bars so many bars—

Clanging.

and chains up the doors he's locked and barred—

Fugue of locking up noises; Pantaleone tittering.

that the house becomes a veritable impregnable fortress.

One final bar clangs.

PUSS. Not to be taken by force, that's for certain! But, perhaps, by guile and stealth, the well-known specialities of the feline kind.

TABS. Even so, inside this maximum security prison, there's the dreadful guardian of the angel . . .

HAG. (*Shattering sneeze.*)

PUSS. The hag. Who is impervious to our furry charms, Tabs.

Room acoustic.

HAG. You get out from under my feet, you pestilential feline, or I'll have your horrible striped hide for dusters—

Blows; squawking of cat; scurrying of paws. Back to close acoustic.

PUSS. Problems, problems, problems . . . yet, dear Tabs, see how my ingenuity rises to this challenge even here in the coal hole, see how my ingenuity rises to this challenge!

TABS. And not only your ingenuity.

Purring.

PUSS. My dearest Tabs . . . do you think . . . if I procured a letter to your mistress from my handsome and charming young master . . . you could . . . slip it to her?

TABS. Watch your language! (*Giggles.*)

PUSS. . . . drat these boots . . .

Fade rustling, clink of coals, purring.

Fade in hero's room, scratching of pen-nib.

HERO. 'Since mine eyes were first dazzled by your beauty, as by the rays of the sun, dear lady . . .' Oh, God!

PUSS. That's not the high road to the rumpling of the bedcovers, sir! She's got one ninny between them already; do you think she wants another?

HERO. When I want your advice, Puss, I shall ask for it.

Rustle of paper; scribble, scribble, scribble. Puss jumps up.

Puss—what are you doing on my knee? You're covered in coal dust, too—get down at once! Get down—you're covered in coal dust and you're jogging my arm, you'll make me blot the paper—there! Now look what you've done . . .

PUSS. (*Aside.*) And never did a missive more deserve to be blotted! Poetry. He's descended to *poetry*! Must the prime symptom of love be always softening of the brain? (*To hero.*) I declare, look what you've written: 'Shall I compare thee to a summer's day . . . '

What? Tell her she resembles a wet Bank Holiday Monday? Do you think that will endear yourself to her? No, no, no, no, no! Where's the true voice of feeling, man—speak from the heart! Tell her all about yourself—

HERO. But—Puss, I'm . . . little better than a petty criminal, Puss. A lecher. A—

PUSS. All good women have a missionary streak, sir. Persuade her she's your salvation and she's yours.

Pause.

HERO. My past . . . my wicked, wicked life . . .

PUSS. Be fair, sir, "wicked" is laying it on a bit thick, sir.

HERO. But, if I could win the love of a good woman, the healing, purifying love of a good woman . . .

Scribble; scribbling fades during following speech:

' . . . a cashiered officer, a card-sharp, a profligate, a wastrel, a cruel, heartless seducer and, if I never stooped to theft, myself, then I was quite content to let my valet do the thieving for me . . . '

Crossfade to heroine's room.

HEROINE. ' . . . but then I saw your face, just for a single moment in the square, and for the first time I knew there was such a thing as forgiveness.'

'Your eyes, like holy candles, your mouth as if its shape was formed by prayer . . . and now, can you credit it, I haunt the church and not the brothel. I pass by on the other side of the street from the taverns and the gambling halls. My life has narrowed down to those few sacred hours a week when I can see the veiled angel who will lead me to grace and bliss.'

Well!

Oh, my dear Tabs! I never meant to wreak such havoc with a heart when I first smiled to see a booted cat!

Sympathetic mew; rustle of letter.

I'll kiss your signature, you poor soul . . . Lelio . . . can his name truly be Lelio? Fate! Fate! And store your letter . . . here . . . in my bodice; yes, where the hag can't find it . . . next to my heart . . .

Rustle.

Oh, the dear, good soul that wrote me such a letter! I am too much in love with virtue to withstand you . . . providing, of course, he's not as ugly as sin or as old as the hills, eh, Tabs, dear?

They laugh.

Clean in hero's room.

PUSS. The lady's tabby confidante entrusted me with this.

HERO. Let's have it—

Rips open envelope.

' . . . never would have believed . . . moved me to the heart . . . '

HEROINE. (*On slight echo.*) ' . . . yet how can I usefully discuss your passion further without a good look at your person?'

Letter clasped.

HERO. I'll serenade her this very evening! Puss, off you go and pawn my sword!

PUSS. Pawn your sword?
(*Aside.*) What does he want to pawn his sword for? what fresh madness is this . . . I knew it! I suspected it! he's going to dress up in costume! Oh, the embarrassment! Oh, unbearable!
(*Narrating.*) For would you credit it, the poor, lovesick buffoon went and bought the white, baggy rags off the back of one of the mountebanks that strut and primp in the square . . . the zany, moonstruck loon, he thought he'd score a bullseye if he played Pierrot . . .

Fade in, very slowly, during ensuing speech, sounds of a street market.

So, when she came out to take her nightly airing at just the hour, the very hour, when they take down the market stalls . . .

Street market; plus clatter of dismantling; bang, crash, donkeys braying, horses whinnying, wheels on cobbles; fade down sufficient for speech to be heard.

. . . out we set across the square.

HERO. There she is! Do you see her? She looks as if she were dreaming, dreaming of me, perhaps . . . what is she looking at? I can't see—I can just see her eyes above her veil but—

PUSS. She's looking at the sickle moon over Bergamo. Strike up.

Guitar introduction; bring up street noises; guitar is lost among them. Stops.

She didn't hear a note. Try again.

Guitar introduction, again.

HERO. (*Sings first phrase of song.*)

Fade up street noises. Song stops.

PUSS. Not heard a word nor turned her head, never caught hair nor hide of you. She's lost, quite lost, in her own sweet thoughts. You might as well have stayed at home and saved your money. Our money.

HERO. Up you go—tell her I'm here.

PUSS. WHAT?

HERO. Up to her window. 'Rococo's a piece of cake,' you said.

PUSS. That ain't rococo, that's Palladian!

TABS. (*Calling.*) Mr Marmalade! Ginger-winger! Here I am! Up on the gutter! Go on, you can do it! See that bloody great caryatid by the door jamb? Just swarm up her loincloth and take it from there!

PUSS. (*Narrating.*) . . . and since my girl was watching me . . .

Fade street noises to background and bring up heavy, effortful breathing and scrape of climbing equipment on stone.

(*Effort.*) . . . from loincloth up . . . to these massy pects . . . but, oh! that Doric column this caryatid upholds . . . never a handhold nor a foothold on a Doric column, dammit . . .

TABS. (*Slightly off.*)What about a flying leap? Are you an acrobat or are you not! Take a flying leap, like Harlequin on wires! Flex your muscles, tense your thighs, and *spring*! You can make it if you really try, I know you can!

PUSS. Right. For my Tabs I'll do it. Very well.
(*Narrating.*) . . . and, with one magnificent upward bound . . .

Whizz of rocket going off.

TABS. Hooray!

PUSS. (*Narrating.*) . . . I landed on the window-sill.

Click of bootheels, landing.

HEROINE. Dear God. What an apparition.

PUSS. Where's the hag?

HEROINE. Sped to the privy, seized with a flux, something she ate . . .

PUSS. What luck.

TABS. (*Sotto voce.*) Luck had nothing to do with it.

PUSS. Quick as you can, cast your eye directly into the square below, ma'am. Him you wot off lurks there in the big hat, in white, ready to sing you an evening ditty—

Door opens off; sneeze.

HAG. (*Off.*) What's going on—THAT CAT!

HEROINE. Scram, Puss!

PUSS. Discretion is the better part—
Whee!

Reversed sound of rocket going off.

(*Narrating.*) Straight out of the window I jumped.

TABS. I don't believe it. It ain't true. My eyes deceive me. No—he's doing it! he's really doing it! He's DONE IT! THE TRIPLE SOMERSAULT!

The reversed rocket sound makes three loops, simulating three somersaults—this during Tabs's speech.

Hurrah! Hurrah! Hurrah! What a cat! What a marmalade marvel! Splendissimo!

PUSS. (*Narrating.*) The triple accident, performed during that three storey drop to the ground—performed, I'm forced to admit, in a not entirely voluntary manner, but not a word to Tabs, the triple somersault left me exhilarated, if breathless.

But did my master so much as witness my triumph, let alone congratulate?

Did he, be blowed.

Bring up street background.

HERO. And now I see her eyes turned towards me, how they shine . . .

Take street noises down as the guitar introduction is played; hero's song—something suitable (tenor)—perhaps something by Benjamin Britten accompanied by Julian Bream. Pause when the song is over; then murmurs of appreciation, patter of applause.

HEROINE. (*Off.*) My dear . . .

HAG. (*Off.*) Back in your box!

Slam—shutters or windows, it doesn't matter; but the slam does: Bang!

Pause.

Fade in hero's room. Mealtime chink of china.

HERO. Bread and cheese? Is there nothing in the house to eat but bread and cheese?

PUSS. Poor pickings, today, sir, but it's weeks since you showed any appetite and I thought—

HERO. Did you hear how she called, 'my dear'? Is there any more of this . . . excellent . . . gorgonzola? (*Chewing.*) I need to keep . . . my strength up, now!

PUSS. (*Huff.*) If you want any more gorgonzola, you can go and pinch it yourself. You know where the grocer's is.

HERO. (*Conciliatory.*) Puss . . .

PUSS. Oh, don't mind me, sir. You just get on with your supper, sir. But don't you believe that tonight's successful serenade marks more than Phase One of the strategy of the siege of Casa Pantaleone!

In fact, if you can do without me for half an hour, sir, I think I'll just slip across the square for a tactical conference in the coal hole with my little fifth columnist . . .

Fade.

Clean in close acoustic.

TABS. Rats!

PUSS. Rats?

TABS. If there's one thing the hag hates more than cats, it's rats. Allergic to cats she may be but with rats she's plain hysterical.

Fade in, briefly, hag screaming, whimpering, gibbering, on echo.

Now, my love, if I was to go, we was to go out hunting together and gather up an enormous number of rats, some killed dead, but some we had merely crippled, so they could still scamper, if slowly, and were we to strew some of these rats around the house but assemble still more of them in, under and around the missus' own bed, one Wednesday morning, after the old fool's gone off about his business, and if you and your young man was to . . .

Fade.

Clean in hero's room.

PUSS. Item one: one houseful of rats;
Item two: one hag in terror of same;
Item three: one young lady confined to her bed for fear of rats;
Item four: one lusty young rat-catcher, to whit, you, sir, in thick disguise, perhaps equipped with a luxuriant and aggressive false moustache so that the hag won't recognise you from church, this rat-catcher plus his intrepid assistant; plying for hire in the square tomorrow morning at just the psychologically precise moment as item two issues from the front door of item one howling, screeching and ululating . . .

Terrible screams.

HAG. Help! Assistance! Help!

Bring in square background behind screams.

HERO. What seems to be the trouble, my good lady?

HAG. Rattus domesticus dead in bed and worse! Ho, horrors, horrors, horrors! Rats everywhere—black rats, brown rats, little rats, big rats! (*Screams.*)

HERO. Allow me to introduce myself; I am nobody but Il Signor

Furioso, professionally known as 'The Living Death of Rats', the sworn enemy of vermin, dedicated to stamping out all the genus of the rattus and the mus variety . . .
(*Sotto voce.*) Have I got the patter right, Puss?

PUSS. (*Sotto voce.*) Spot on.

HERO. Lead us directly to the site of the infestation.

HAG. (*Screams. Then sneezes.*) Can't you leave that cat behind?

HERO. What? Venture on an invasion without my assistant, my partner, my pal, my very own ambulant rat trap, my sworn lieutenant in the fight against rattus domesticus, rattus rattus and last but not least tiny wee mus musculus—

HAG. Oh, stop it! stop it! Just to hear you name the beasts sets me all of a shake—come quick!

Speeded up footsteps; on flagstones of hall; lose street background; feet stop.

HERO. (*Sotto voce.*) I say, Puss, haven't you overdone it a bit? The house is like a museum of rats . . .

Faint squeaking; footsteps up stairs.

PUSS. Trust your faithful servant, sir . . .

HEROINE. (*Off—calls.*) Have your found a rat-catcher? I daren't get out of bed in case I tread on one of the beasts—

Bedroom door opens; squeaks! Over to heroine's bedroom.

PUSS. (*Aside.*) Rats a-plenty, all alive oh; and there she is, the beauty, up on the bed with the covers up to her chin, and everywhere you look a heaving sea, rattus, rattus, rattus—

Squeaks; screams; sneezes.

HAG. Curse the rats! Drat the cat!

PUSS. . . . although, of course, none of the ratti in the best of health, more the atmosphere of a rat casualty ward, in here, than a rat holiday camp . . .

HERO. Good morning, signora! In a moment, all your prayers will be answered. Allow me to introduce myself, Il Signor Furioso and his toothed, clawed, vermin exterminator.

HEROINE. Haven't we met somewhere before, Puss?

HERO. See! Over there, Puss! that big, black beast! Pounce, Puss, pounce!

Terrified squeak; tearing, rending, gobbling.

HEROINE. Oh, Signor Furioso, what are you doing under the bed?

HERO. (*Muffled.*) Just . . . taking a look . . . I knew it! Here, in the wainscotting, the biggest hole I ever saw . . . and a detachment, a battalion, an army of the biggest, blackest rats you ever did see lining up behind it ready to storm through!

HAG. (*Shrieks. Then sneezes.*) I'll expire directly!

HEROINE. You go and recover yourself in the kitchen over an infusion of friar's balsam—don't come back until it's over.

PUSS. (*Narrating.*) I can tell the hag is torn between the extreme terror and discomfort of her present situation and loyalty to her employer etc. etc. etc. What? Leave the young lady alone? With her legs unshackled? In a bedroom? With a man? So the hag dithers and shilly shallies until I lob her a little brown mouse, still twitching, with a quick flick of the left paw, it strikes her straight on the chin—

HAG. (*Screams.*)

Feet run; door slams.

HEROINE. Just . . . lock the door . . .

Key turns; squeaks die down.

Fade in, very softly, reprise of hero's serenade.

HERO. I hardly dare . . . to take your hand . . .

HEROINE. Then I . . . must take yours.

HERO. My darling!

HEROINE. My dearest . . .

HERO. As if we were made for one another . . .

PUSS. (*Sotto voce.*) Come off it, sir; do you think she thinks you've staged this grand charade solely in order to kiss her hand?

And get that false moustache off, pronto, love may not consort with the ludicrous . . .

HEROINE. Perhaps . . . we might remove the hairy evidence of Signor Furioso from your upper lip?

HERO. Oh . . . the false moustache . . . there. Is that better?

HEROINE. All the better to kiss me with.

HERO. Too much . . .

PUSS. (*Sotto voce.*) Get a move on, you two! Full speed ahead! Do you want the hag to catch you in flagrante?

HEROINE. Don't you think we'd be more comfortable . . . prone?

HERO. My dearest—

Puss! Puss! Mimic the murder of rats immediately! Mask the music of Venus with the clamour of Diana!

PUSS. Tantivvy!

Squeaks; bedsprings; hunting horns; male voice choir sings 'A-Hunting We Will Go!'; male and female sighing; battering on door.

HAG. (*Off.*) I say, I say, I say! What's going on? Whyfor the racket?

PUSS. (*Over.*) But did they answer? Did they, like hell.

Slowly fade effects and mix with gratified laughter of the lovers; bang, bang, bang on door; unlocking.

HEROINE. See what a victory there's been! The rats are all dead, every one! Oh, Signor Furioso, how can I ever thank you enough? And as for you, you valiant Puss—

HAG. Atishoo! What's all this mess, what's been going on, why are the bedclothes in such a tangle, and the sheet's been ripped . . .

HEROINE. Such deeds as took place on that bed, governess! If the mattress could only speak, it would provide such credentials to the courage and capacity of Signor Furioso . . . and, Signor, how much do we owe you for your singular services?

HERO. Owe me? Why, not a—

PUSS. (*Prompt.*) One hundred ducats. (*Sotto voce.*) What, do it for nothing, would you, you honourable idiot?

HEROINE. Only one hundred ducats?

HAG. That's the entire household expenses for a month!

HEROINE. And worth every penny! Wouldn't the rats have eaten us out of house and home, by then? Go on, go and fetch the money, no need to mention it to my husband; you can easily spare a hundred ducats out of the cash you skim off the housekeeping, hag.
      Can't she, Puss?

      Purr.

HAG. What's this? Atishoo! Get this horrid thing off me, go away—

HEROINE. A hundred ducats. Fetch. Or else the cat will cling on to you like a burr, like a tick, like a succubus—

      Sneezes diminish as if the babbling hag is running down a corridor; soft laughter and much purring; fade.

PUSS. (*Narrating.*) So that night we sat down to a supper for which, for the first time in some months, mere circumstances had not dictated the menu but all honestly bought from shops . . .

      Fade in hero's room. Clink of cutlery and china.

Eat up, sir. Such a nice escaloppe de veau and you ain't touched it! Nor the mushrooms, neither, not that I fancy fungi myself, but you've always hitherto relished a—

      Knife and fork flung aside.

Can't fancy it? But you ate like a horse after she smiled at you— (*Aside.*) now he picks like a bird after he—I don't understand the human heart, and that's the truth.

HERO. (*Laughs. This has nothing to do with Puss; he is quite preoccupied.*)

PUSS. What's the joke? Share it with Puss.

HERO. (*Weeps.*)

PUSS. (*Aside.*) And now he's burst out crying . . . what's got into him? Is he sickening for something? Could he have picked a germ up from the rats?

    Still, no point in wasting that bit of veal . . .

HERO. I must and will have her for ever!

PUSS. (*Chokes on mouthful. Aside.*) That fairly put me off my supper, too. I see how satisfaction has not satisfied him. I therefore push my plate aside and fall to grooming myself meditatively. (*Licking.*) Unusually grimy about the shirt-front . . . hmm . . . strong flavour of coal dust about my person . . .

HERO. How can I live without her?

PUSS. (*In the midst of washing himself.*) You've done so . . . for twenty five years, sir . . . and never missed her for a moment . . .

HERO. I'm burning with the fever of love!

PUSS. Then we're spared the expense of fires.

HERO. I shall snatch her away from her husband and we'll live together, always!

PUSS. What do you propose to live on?

HERO. (*Distracted.*) Kisses . . . embraces . . .

PUSS. Well, you won't grow fat on *that*, sir, though *she* will, and then there'll be more mouths to feed.

HERO. (*Turning on him.*) I'm sick and tired of your foul-mouthed barbs, Puss!

PUSS. (*Huff.*) Sorry. Sorry I spoke, sir. Pardon me for breathing, sir. My apologies for living, sir. Huh. That's gratitude for you. Pshaw!

    Jumps to floor with a thump; imperious mewing.

Let me out! Open that door!

    Door opens smartly.

HERO. Good riddance!

Door slam. Cut to close acoustic of coal hole.

TABS. Had your supper, have you?

PUSS. . . . the merest snack . . .

TABS. Because I've saved you this pig's trotter the missus smuggled me. 'For services rendered,' she said, and tipped me such a wink.

PUSS. I think I could manage a pig's trotter. (*Chewing.*)

TABS. And she was in ever such a funny mood. First she laughed like a mad thing and then all at once she's April, with the showers—how she cried!

'How can I live without him?' she demands, but does not wait for an answer. 'I must and will have him for ever,' she declares. And the next breath vows she'll leave her husband. Did you ever hear such things?

PUSS. (*Swallows last mouthful.*) I heard them just this minute, Tabs. It's plain enough these two speak with one voice the plain, clear, foolish rhetoric of love.

TABS. (*Sentimental sigh.*)

PUSS. Yes.

Pause.

TABS. But only *we* are smart enough to bring them together! Scheme, Mr Marmalade, scheme!

PUSS. Tabs, my dearest . . . slowly recapitulate for me the daily motions of Signor Pantaleone, alias old Pantaloon, when he's at home.

Fade in church bell ringing four as Tabs speaks.

TABS. (*Narrating.*) They set the clock of the duomo by him, so rigid and regular is he in his habits. Up at the crack—

Cock-crow; Pantaleone makes waking-up grunts.

He makes a meagre breakfast off yesterday's crusts . . .

Gnawing at stale bread.

PANTALEONE. (*In room acoustic.*) Bread's tough, this morning . . .

TABS. . . . which he dips to soften 'em in a cup of cold water—

Water poured out.

that he drinks cold, to spare the expense of a fire. Then, bright and early, down to the counting-house—

PANTALEONE. Good morrow to my gold!

TABS. —counting out the money—

Chink, chink, chink; Pantaleone giggles and babbles with glee.

until a well-earned bowl of water gruel, that is, water extravagantly *boiled*, served hot—

PANTALEONE. (*Smacks lips.*) That's the stuff!

TABS. —at midday. His afternoons he devotes to usury, bank-rupting here—

SMALL TRADESMAN. I'm ruined. You devil!

TABS. —a small businessman; there, a weeping widow.

WIDOW. My starving children! My roofless orphans!

TABS. All this he does for fun and profit, both. Which puts him in the mood for a luxurious dinner prompt at four—more piping hot water, with perhaps a bit of rancid beef in it, or a rubber hen, or some such, he's got an arrangement with the butcher—

PANTALEONE. Tee hee! my old bird for his old bird; take his unsold stock off his hands, fair exchange, on Friday nights he gets the use of the hag . . .

Affronted noise from hag.

TABS. From four-thirty to five-thirty, while he airs his young wife at the window—

PANTALEONE. —giving the occasional twitch to my big toe to make sure she's safe and sound the while—

HEROINE. (*Off.*) Oh!

TABS. —he himself adjourns to his strong-room, to check out his chests of gems, his bales of silk, the Persian carpets he keeps well rolled up and out of sight, since, like the missus, they are too beautiful to waste on the eyes of the *hoi polloi.*

Pantaleone exclaiming over his treasures. Chinks, rustles, etc.

Then—it's early to bed! So as to waste no candles. And sinless slumber in the prospect of another happy today tomorrow.

Pantaleone gives one snore. Fade.

Back to close acoustic.

That is his life.

PUSS. Just how rich is he?

TABS. Croesus.

PUSS. Sufficient to support two loving couples?

TABS. Sumptuous.

PUSS. My sweet, pretty, clever one, my soubrette in stripes, Susanna to my Figaro and Columbine to my Harlequin . . . ma chère . . . chérie . . . what if, early some uncandled morning, as the old man, bleary with sleep, descends the staircase blind to all but the peckish anticipation of his bread and water . . . what if, what if then he were to place his foot on the subfusc yet volatile fur of a shadow-camouflaged young tabby cat?

TABS. And topple, topple, topple . . . ? You read my mind, my love.

Fade.

Fade in hero's room.

PUSS. Now, sir, you must raid the hagoness' store of ducats and set yourself up in all the gear of a medical man, for we're going to be disciples of Hippocrates.

HERO. What are you up to now?

PUSS. Do as I say and never mind the reasons. Off you go and fully equip yourself. A black bag, a skull cap—and another dose of facial hair, yes; a grey beard, this time. That'll inspire confidence!

Besides, some sugar pills and bottles of coloured water and jars of goose-grease . . .

HERO. When you've finished with your shopping list—

PUSS. Tomorrow morning, disguised as a doctor, you must stand up proudly in the square for hire, and I, masquerading as your nurse, shall carry the sign. 'Il famoso dottore, aches cured, pains prevented, lovers united, etc. etc. etc.'

HERO. Is she going to play the invalid? Is that the plot? So I can get into her room again? I'll take her in my arms and—jump out of the window with her, we shall perform the triple somersault of love even if we don't outlive it, I—

PUSS. Now, now, now, now, now! Don't let it go to your head, sir. Just leave well alone and do what I say and things will turn out handy dandy, sir. Haven't they up till now?

HERO. (*Grudging.*) I suppose so. May I presume to ask you exactly when we're to have our game of doctors and nurses?

Church bell rings four times; wind blows through square.

(*Shivers.*) . . . Another raw, misty, bleak, angular, comfortless morning, the darkness before dawn . . . but so dark you think the dawn will never come. And surely this winter has lasted all my life?
    So cold, here, out in the square, Puss . . .

PUSS. Nobody about, yet . . . what's that?

Cough.

HERO. A client! We didn't prepare for unexpected clients!

PUSS. Let me handle this. No point in passing up a bob or two, is there.

Cough.

COUGHER. Got anything for a hacking cough?

PUSS. Rub this on your chest, mate. Ten ducats.

Tin unscrewed.

COUGHER. Coo! what a pong! What the 'ell is this? Gone off, 'as it? Ten ducats for this?

PUSS. Oh, no, no, no, my good man! It ain't never gone off! The miraculous substance in this little tin is a triple distilled ointment prepared from the highly refined, ah, lard, of the left thigh of the, ah, exceedingly rare, prophylactically valuable, newly discovered American *armadillo*—

COUGHER. Armadillos? What's armadillos got to do with a hacking cough? And what's more, I don't like the look of your whiskers. Nor, so help me God, of that long red *tail* of yours. I think you've got charlatan written all over you. Take back your lousy unguent!

HERO. Come, come, my good fellow; my assistant, trained in Bologna—

COUGHER. Crooks!

Door flies open; weeping.

HAG. (*Off.*) Is there a doctor in the house! Doctor! Oh, doctor, come at once! Our good man's taken a sorry tumble!

Hag weeps ostentatiously; speeded up footsteps onto flag-stones; lose square background.

HERO. Where's the patient?

HAG. At the stairfoot.

PUSS. Ah!

HEROINE. Are you the doctor? My husband—a fall—

HERO. Puss, my bag . . .

HEROINE. Puss? You, again? Oh—

Stifles a giggle.

HERO. Where's my little mirror . . . just hold it to his lips . . .

HAG. Dead, is he? Broke his neck, did he? Where's the keys to the counting house—

HEROINE. Surely I detect the faintest misting of the glass? Enough to give hope? Oh, doctor, we must carry him up to bed and make him comfortable . . .

HERO. Hup!

Heaves up a dead weight.

PUSS. (*Narrating.*) The master, nothing loath, pops Pantaloon over his shoulder in a fireman's lift and the entire party repair to the bedroom in two shakes of a bee's wagger, the young lady pretty as a picture in her morning negligee and keeping, I notice, a weather eye open on the activities of the hag, who's blubbering like a stuck pig to conceal they way she's hovering round the defunct miser and making little darting sallies at his pockets with her thieving hands—

Clean in bedroom.

HEROINE. She's after the keys to the counting house. Take that!

Slap.

HAG. Ouch!

HERO. There . . .

Flop of body on bed.

Hmm . . . no heartbeat that I can hear . . . and when I tap his knee with my little hammer—

Tap.

—no reflex. I hold his wrist and feel no pulse. And when I slip my hand into his wife's bodice—

HEROINE. (*Sighs.*)

HERO. —not the flicker of an eyelid. Dead as a doornail. It's not a doctor you want for this one, madame; it's an undertaker.

HEROINE. Off you go and fetch one, hag. This minute!

HAG. Let's just see how much he's worth, first—go on. Just give me the keys to the counting-house—

HEROINE. I forethoughtfully removed them from his belt while you went to find a doctor, hag.

Jangle of flourished keys.

See! We'll check out the counting-house the minute the cover's nailed down on him!

HAG. The minute?

HEROINE. The instant. Undertaker first. *Then* counting-house.

HAG. (*Sneezes.*) Blasted cat back again . . . undertaker, first. Then counting house. All right. Very well. Undertaker first . . .

Scuttles off; door slam.

HEROINE. Darling!

HERO. Dearest!

HEROINE. Get that . . . false beard off . . .

Embrace.

The bed—

HEROINE. Occupied.

HERO. The floor—

They fall down.

PUSS. (*Discreet cough.*) If a veil were to hand, I would now draw it to conceal the embraces of these two young lovers; but, as it is, I must ask you to exercise the same discretion as Puss himself, who now opened the shutters—

Shutters open.

and unbarred the windows—

Unbarring.

—and slipped out onto the balcony to observe the rosy fingers of the dawn, for, during the time we had been busy with Signor Pantaleone, those fingers had painted they sky with a veritable herbacious border.

Dawn chorus.

A lovely morning, full of the joyous beginnings of spring; the voice of the turtles . . .

TABS. What'cher, Ginger! Hark at the birdies! Delicious!

PUSS. I do believe at last that winter is over and gone.

Can't you smell a *green* smell, a fragrance of burgeoning things, of quickening—

TABS. 'Burgeoning' and 'quickening' is right, Ginge. For, oh, my love! I do have the most momentous secret to whisper in your ear—

PUSS. A secret?

TABS. Bend down . . .

Whispers.

PUSS. Really and truly?

TABS. No more than Nature's way. But now your rambling days are over, lad. No more nights on the tiles for you—

PUSS. —no moonlight serenades—

TABS. —sing lullabies, instead. And, henceforward, we two shall sit one on each side of the parlour mantlepiece, as if we were cats made out of china, the household ornaments, Mr and Mrs Marmalade . . .

PUSS. . . . Puss and his Tabby, the genii of the home and the protectors of the hearth. Yes. Well, chérie, my most chérie, few have worked as hard to achieve the tranquil joys of domesticity as you and I. Won't you snuggle up a little closer, Tabs? Plenty of room on the windowsill . . .

Fade in Rossini's cat duet; and, at the same time . . .

HERO. Dearest.

HEROINE. Darling.

Passionate breathing.

PUSS. (*Narrating.*) And, at just this tender if outrageous moment—

Door bursts open. Bedroom acoustic.

UNDERTAKER. In comes I, the undertaker, with a brace of mutes—

MUTES. (*Mumble, mumble.*)

UNDERTAKER. —the mutes bearing between them a nice, comfy box of elm, good old, solid elm. And what greets our eyes?

MUTES. (*Excited mumbles.*)

UNDERTAKER. Why, a handsome young couple naked as nature intended, stretched out on the carpet and at it hammer and tongs!
Hurrah!
Magnificent!

Cheers and applause.

The mutes applaud and make enthusiastic, if inarticulate, cries; torrent of applause and cheers; fade in climax of Tchaikovsky's 1812 Overture, with cannons; shattering climax; thunderous applause.

Pause.

Spectacular. Spectacular . . . well done, sir and madame.

HAG. Thieves! Murder! Fornication!

HEROINE. (*Firm.*) That's quite enough of your nonsense, hag. New brooms sweep clean. Go and pack your bags.

HAG. What's this? Going to turn me out, are you? After what I did with the butcher to put meat in the pot? Thieves! Murder! Fornication!

HEROINE. Indeed I shall give you the sack, hag, but I'll stuff it with money, first, don't you worry. Yet how can I retain you in my house when your sneezes cause such suffering to my beloved cats?
And, hag, remember . . . it's MY house, now. And my counting-house. For now I am a rich widow and here—

PUSS. (*Narrating.*)—and with a flourish of the counting-house keys she indicates my bare yet blissful master—

HEROINE. —here's the young man who'll be my second husband!

Renewed applause and cheers; wedding bells; wedding march on organ.

PUSS. (*Narrating.*) And so I took my master the quickest way to a happy ending; and the young missus rounding out already. But my Tabs beat her to it, since cats don't take half so much lazy time about bringing their progeny into the world as *homo sapiens* does, so almost before they've cleared away the wedding breakfast there's three fine new-minted kittens taking their bows—

Mew.

Mew.

Mew.

—all as marmalade as might be and each equipped with the snowiest of dickeys, who tumble in the cream pan—

Splash.

and tangle up the missus' knitting—

Sounds of irritation.

and tumble about the parquet flooring like the born acrobats they are—

Kitten mewing, skidding—whee!

—and put a smile on every face, especially those of their proud mother and father.

So, ladies and gentlemen, all is set fair. And may I wish you goodnight and sweet dreams.

And let me wish you, too, in parting, as follows: that all your wives, if you need them, be rich and pretty; and all your husbands, if you want them, be young and virile; and all your cats as wily, resourceful and perspicacious as—PUSS IN BOOTS.

Fade in conclusion of Figaro's aria.

CHALLENGING FICTION

Jenny Joseph
Persephone
When Persephone returns from the underworld, winter releases its grip on the earth. Jenny Joseph sets this timeless story of good and evil in both the ancient and the modern world.

B.S. Johnson
House Mother Normal
Anthony Burgess called B.S. Johnson 'the only British author with the guts to reassess the novel form, extend its scope and still work in a recognisable fictional tradition'. *House Mother Normal* was his fifth and finest novel.

Shena Mackay
An Advent Calendar
'Shena Mackay's talent is to put the ruth back into ruthless rhymes. Her novels are visions of universal anguish . . . Funny, terrifying, and written by an angel' — BRIGID BROPHY

Eva Figes
Days
'*Days* has a kind of violent stillness, great turbulence beneath a surface calm . . .It's extraordinary how much this gifted writer manages to pack into her austere frame' — *Guardian*

David Constantine
Davies
Davies was famous for a moment in 1911 when Home Secretary Winston Churchill raised his case in the House of Commons. But who was Davies? In this fictionalised account of a lifelong petty criminal, Constantine unravels the mystery of a shadowy loner caught in a vicious circle of self-perpetuating crime.

For a complete list of Bloodaxe publications write to: Bloodaxe Books Ltd, P.O. Box 1SN, Newcastle upon Tyne NE99 1SN.

BLOODAXE BOOKS